BETTER BRIDGE WITH A BETTER MEMORY

How Mnemonics Will Improve Your Game

Two distinct memory areas are involved in bridge. Your long-term memory houses your bidding system, your knowledge of card combinations, opening leads, signals, declarer technique and defensive strategy. Your short-term memory handles the deal in progress: the bidding, the lead, the cards that have been played, which cards are high and so on.

Each bridge deal lasts about 6-7 minutes. When the deal is over, your short-term memory has to wipe the slate clean and start the process anew for the next deal. The fresher you are, the higher the level of your concentration and the more efficient your short-term memory. In addition, the more efficient your long-term memory, the less energy is needed to recall such details and consequently more energy is at your disposal to fuel your short-term memory. A strong long-term memory leads to a more powerful short-term memory.

Improve Your Bridge Memory provided techniques for enhancing both your long-term and your short-term memory. *Better Bridge with a Better Memory* is designed to strengthen your long-term memory, both in regard to the conventions you use and the strategy recommended for best results in the bidding, declarer play and defence. By the use of mnemonics, easily recalled phrases, catchwords or acronyms, you will be able to strengthen your long-term memory. As these recollections become easier and easier, your short-term memory will be sharper and your concentration will last longer. The benefits will appear in the improved results you obtain.

Ron Klinger has written over thirty bridge books and has played for Australia on numerous occasions, including the Bermuda Bowl in 1976, 1989 and 1993 and the World Open Teams Olympiad in 1976, 1980, 1984 and 1988. His international wins include the South Pacific Teams, the Far East Teams and the Far East Pairs (twice). He won the Bols Brilliancy Prize for best play at the 1976 world championships and has won two Bols prizes for journalism.

BETTER BRIDGE WITH A BETTER MEMORY

How Mnemonics Will Improve Your Game

Ron Klinger

LONDON

VICTOR GOLLANCZ

in association with

PETER CRAWLEY

First published in Great Britain 1998
in association with Peter Crawley
by Victor Gollancz
An imprint of the Cassell Group
Wellington House, 125 Strand, London WC2R 0BB

A catalogue record for this book
is available from the British Library

ISBN 0 575 06536 2

Typeset in Australia by Modern Bridge Publications,
60 Kameruka Road, Northbridge, NSW 2063, Australia

Printed in Great Britain by
St Edmundsbury Press Ltd, Bury St Edmunds, Suffolk

To Pat Husband

With affection

CONTENTS

INTRODUCTION

This book owes its existence to Dr. Sean Hoban of Ireland. I am indebted to Sean for the concept and for his ideas and assistance in this project. Sean originally wrote to me that when he was studying medicine at university, he found mnemonics invaluable in being able to recall anatomy, physiology, symptoms, diagnoses and treatments. 'I can still reel off the 12 cranial nerves because of a mnemonic and rhyme I learned in 1951,' he wrote. Sean sent me some books on Mnemonics for Medics and a request for a similar book for bridge players. 'Would you please write one?' This book is the outcome. Thank you, Sean.

****

How many experts, top class players, do you think there are in your country? How many are strong enough to represent their country in international competition? In Australia there are 30,000 registered players. England has about the same.

I would have great difficulty in trying to fill 50 top class Australian teams, to find 300 players who could legitimately be classed experts. Let's suppose I am unduly cynical, excessively critical, and there are really twice as many experts as that. 600 experts in England or Australia would represent only 2% of the total number of registered players. I doubt that any country would boast a higher percentage.

That leaves 98% of the bridge population whose game can do with an uplift. These players do not aspire to be champions but want to play at a competent standard, to play well and enjoy the game without making mickey-mouse blunders. It is impossible to be perfect at the game (and thus very frustrating if you are a perfectionist) but you can achieve a standard to be proud of if you are prepared to put in some effort.

This book is for those of the 98% who feel limited by their memory and the finite nature of their mind, for those who seek an easier way to remember what matters. No one need be saddled with a bad memory. You can improve recall through mnemonics to trigger the appropriate action in many situations This means not only for the system you play but also the principles for winning, whether in the bidding, the opening lead, declarer play or defence. What you need to improve your game is the desire, the motivation, the drive and the will to succeed.

This book covers various routes to winning bridge. Not only is the right strategy presented but also an easy way to remember it. No apology is made for stating the key concepts again and again. Repetition is to memory what training is to athletics. Repetition will ensure that the ideas are soundly implanted and easily recalled. Hopefully, you will find some fresh ideas in this book. At the very least, principles of sound bidding, play and defence will be reinforced.

Once you see the approach, you can devise your own memory aids, your own mnemonics. Indeed, if you come up with an effective mnemonic, I would be delighted to hear from you (see below).

Apply a recall strategy as soon as you have read the relevant section. You need not cover everything before enjoying the fruits of your labour.

After completing the book and putting all or most of the ideas into practice, you will experience the satisfaction of knowing you are doing the right thing, even if this does not result in a tangible reward every time. Your game is bound to improve and you will score more wins.

That will be pleasant enough but an even bigger bonus awaits you. Once the principles are part and parcel of your long-term memory, you can go forward and further, beyond the memory-aids. You will discover there is much more, a new frontier of bridge. This new challenge will be savoured, relished, appreciated, enjoyed. Then I will be delighted to welcome you to the world of . . .

Happy bridging.

Ron Klinger, 1998

Do you have a good bridge mnemonic or what you feel is an improved version of a mnemonic in this book? If so, we would be delighted to hear from you. If your mnemonic is used in a future edition of this book, not only will your contribution be duly acknowledged but we will also be happy to supply you with a copy of the edition in which your mnemonic appears.
Please forward your suggestions to:
> *Ron Klinger,*
> *P.O. Box 140,*
> *Northbridge, NSW 1560,*
> *Australia*

CHAPTER 1

MEMORY, MNEMONICS & BRIDGE

Do you ever forget where you put your keys? Do you go searching for your glasses and find that they were in your hand all the time? Do you vainly try to remember the name of someone to whom you have just been introduced? Do you look up a phone number and just as you start dialling you find you need to look up the number again?

These are common occurrences for most people. The good news is that the problem is virtually never that you have a poor memory or that your memory is failing. The fault almost invariably is that you did not put enough concentration into the matter originally. You failed to make a 'mental note' when you put your keys down, when you picked up your glasses, when the introduction was made, when you read the phone number originally. Had you put sufficient effort into recording the information to start with, you would have had less of a problem recalling it when needed.

The human memory is a most amazing phenomenon with a storage capacity of billions of piece of information, greater than the most modern computers. Nevertheless, we forget. We forget which cards are high, how many trumps have gone, the correct response to an asking bid, the right strategy for the hand that confronts us.

There are three stages of remembering: recording, retaining and recalling. Recording refers to the initial learning of the material. Retaining is storing the information until it needs to be retrieved. Recalling, being able to reproduce the information when needed, is what is generally meant by remembering. The better the initial recording of the material, the more efficient will be the retrieval process.

You would be surprised at how many songs you know the words of, how many poems or nursery rhymes you can repeat even after all these years. It is less surprising when you consider how often you would have repeated the words of popular songs or rhymes. The constant repetition has made them truly unforgettable.

Likewise, many bridge players can compete effectively and keep on winning in their eighties and nineties. They learnt their good practices originally and have applied them for many years. The skill remains.

A good piece of news is that memory does not have to deteriorate with age. Unless your brain has suffered physical damage, there is no reason why you cannot stay mentally vibrant and alert for the rest of your days. As long as the brain is stimulated, memory need not decay. On the contrary, it can actually improve. And the best piece of news is that bridge is one of the activities which do stimulate the brain.

There are plenty of examples of players performing impressive bridge feats at remarkable ages. World championships have been won by players in their seventies, national championships by players in their eighties and club championships by those in their nineties. In 1997, Jessel Rothfield at age 79 won the South Pacific zonal teams and thus came to represent Australia in the Bermuda Bowl, the world open teams championship. And you could do so too, if you had the same enthusiasm and drive.

A favourite saying for those who do not wish to learn any more: 'You can't teach an old dog new tricks.' A more accurate version is, 'If you have stopped learning new tricks, you have become an old dog.' Plenty of players do not want to try anything new. They are happy to play the same way, day in and day out. They have reached their level and do not want to progress. They are the 'old dogs' of bridge. As you are reading this book, I am pleased to see that you are not one of them.

There are also two distinct memory processes: *short-term memory* and *long-term memory*. 'Short-term memory' refers to how much information you can perceive at the one time. It is similar to the idea of your 'attention span', the amount you are consciously paying attention to at any given time. For a bridge player, short-term memory revolves around the cards you hold, how the bidding went, what the bidding means, which cards have been played and which remain to be played.

The bad news for bridge players is that short-term memory is very short indeed. The forgetting rate of items in short-term memory is between 30 and 90 seconds, while a bridge hand usually lasts between five and seven minutes. No wonder players forget which card their partner played originally, the first discard by an opponent, what suits declarer bid, and so on. Some opponents make it worse than ever for you. By sitting and thinking (and sometimes not thinking, I suspect) for a seeming eternity, they wreak havoc on your short-term memory. In my view, directors are generally too lenient with the snails of bridge.

Concentration is closely linked to the efficiency of your short-term memory. The more powerful your concentration, the longer will the material stay with you. Making a 'mental note' of the important information is a good start. Repetition of the relevant details will implant the 'mental note'.

In order to store the information, you must first receive it. You will often see players deliberately leaving a trick face up for a few seconds. They are storing the information of that trick into their short-term memory. How often have you suddenly wondered at trick 3, 'Which card did partner play at trick 1?' The reason you do not know is that you did not pay attention to that card when it was played. You have not necessarily forgotten the card partner has played. If you did not note it at the time, the information was not received and therefore was not stored at all. It was not there for you to forget.

We see plenty of things we do not notice. I would bet you have seen this information hundreds or thousands of times and yet you cannot give the answer: In an ordinary pack of cards, which jacks are one-eyed? Which kings hold their swords in their left hand? If you do not know, it is not because you have forgotten but rather that you have never paid any attention to these details. Information not stored cannot be recalled.

In order to improve your card memory, you must consciously focus on the card as it is played. If the card is important, repeat the details to yourself, make a mental note. You will find it easier to retrieve the information later if it becomes necessary.

Improving your short-term memory and concentration span appeared in *Improve Your Bridge Memory*. This book is concerned with techniques to enhance your long-term memory.

Long-term memory includes factual information, how to do something (skills, such as riding a bicycle, skating, playing bridge) and events in your personal history. Evidence suggests that everything experienced by your senses is stored and retained. There are virtually no limits to the capacity of your long-term memory and, barring accidents, the contents of your long-term memory are permanent.

The ability to recall the information is related to how well it was learnt originally. The better the filing method, the speedier the retrieval. There are ways to improve your learning techniques and so enhance recall.

Learning and memory both improve if the material is repeated and repeated. There have been many instances when students have told me, 'When I first read your book, I found it very difficult. Now when I read it again, it all makes sense.' Studies indicate that intensive learning greatly assists memory.

If you are playing a complex system or convention, then learning it just sufficiently to play it may be adequate initially, but to retain it for future use requires revision and repetition. If it takes you three attempts to learn a convention, then you will remember it much longer if you repeat it another dozen times.

The more you know about a subject, the easier you will find learning more about it. Enthusiasm for the material is important. If one partner loves to play a complex method and the other partner finds it a chore, guess which one will find it easier to learn? A word of advice: if your partner does not wish to learn a convention, do not force it. A player forced to learn and play a method against his will forgets it in the heat of battle and so 'proves' that the convention was no good after all.

The loss from forgetting a convention is usually much greater than the benefits of playing that convention. The fewer conventions and the simpler your system, the less memory work is involved. In consequence you have more energy for concentration and this will assist your short-term memory.

Mnemonics refers to any memory aid and includes acronyms, alliteration, rhymes, abbreviations and quotations. The mnemonics in this book are mainly of the acronym kind. Some of these form a word, which then becomes the key to recalling. Examples include PRAWNS, SPATS, HURT, FUNDS and MAFIA. In others, the letters do not form any word and therefore the letters are given a secondary meaning, which is easy to remember. For example, **R.T.T.** becomes **R**aise **T**he **T**itanic and remembering or visualising that phrase will help to recall the principle of declarer play to which **R.T.T.** refers. As imagery aids memory, the final chapter suggests ideas to imprint the mnemonic by visualisation.

Learning is made easier by the use of rhymes and alliteration. Will the beginner learn more quickly that the cards are placed on the right after shuffling if the teacher tells the class so, or if the teacher uses a rhyme such as, 'If you would avoid a fight, place the cards upon your right'?

An easy way to remember whether a stopper is shown or denied when playing the Lebensohl convention is via 'Slow Shows' and 'Direct Denies'. Similarly, 'eight ever, nine never' is a handy guide for when to finesse for a missing queen and when to play for the drop, even though there are many reservations about applying that rhyming 'rule'.

Using patterns can make a memory task easier. In a relay system, simple rules are needed to remember the order of hand patterns. For example, if after some earlier bidding, a 2NT rebid shows a 5-3-3-2 pattern with 5 clubs, and 3♣ asks for the precise holdings, the 3♢, 3♡ and 3♠ replies can be used to show 2-3-3-5, 3-2-3-5 and 3-3-2-5 patterns. You can quickly spot the rule that applies here, either 'high-shortage-first' or even simpler, show patterns in numerical order: 2335/3235/3325.

When creating or learning a system, try to make as many areas as similar as possible. Bidding after a 2♣ : 2♢, 2NT rebid should be the same as after a 2NT opening in order to make recall easier. Likewise, for memory's sake, the bidding structure after a 1NT overcall should differ as little as possible from bidding after a 1NT opening.

A sound principle of teaching is to relate something new to something already familiar. For example,

A. NORTH	**B.** NORTH	**C.** NORTH
10 5 2	A 9 2	J 6 5
EAST	EAST	EAST
K J 9 4	Q 10 8 3	A Q 10 2

If switching to this suit, which card should East lead? With dummy on your right and a high card in dummy surrounded (the J-9 surround dummy's 10 in A) plus a higher non-touching honour in your hand as well, *visualise dummy's surrounded card in your own hand. That gives you a sequence and the correct card to lead is top of the sequence.* Thus, the teacher uses a familiar concept (leading top of a sequence) to deal with a difficult area ('surround leads'). With this aid, the student can easily find the right lead, jack in A, 10 in B and queen in C.

Learning and performance are also enhanced if you are relaxed. Say to yourself 'I am going to enjoy myself, no matter what' at the start of a session and if you can play calmly and serenely, you are likely to recall things more easily and more quickly. If you want to win, never, never rebuke your partners. It does not make them play better. On the contrary,

CHAPTER 2

CONVENTIONS & MNEMONICS

Some acronyms for conventions can be very useful since they indicate how the convention is to be used. Thus the name itself triggers the memory. Others are useless in this regard. For example, ASTRO comes from **A**llinger – **St**ern – **Ro**sler, the inventors of the convention, but this gives no clue as to how Astro works. Similarly, D.O.N.T. (**D**isturbing **O**pponent's **N**o-**T**rump, also known as Bergen over no-trumps), S.O.A.P. (**S**ystem **O**ver **A**rtificial **P**re-emption) or NAMYATS (Stayman backwards, a convention about strong, artificial 4♣ and 4◇ openings) may be clever but convey no information as to the structure of the methods advocated.

These conventions include details of the structure within the name itself:

CRASH is a method for showing two-suiters and was originally devised by Kit Woolsey and Steve Robinson as a defensive structure against strong 1♣ openings. The suits shown can be two of the same **C**olour (red suits *or* black suits), two of the same **R**ank (majors *or* minors) or two of the same **Sh**ape (pointed suits – spades / diamonds – *or* rounded suits – hearts / clubs). Hence **C**-**RA**-**SH**. In the current version, double is **C**olour, 1◇ is **RA**nk and 1NT is **SH**ape. The bids are made on weak hands with good distribution. A 5-5 pattern is excellent but at least a 5-4 or 4-4-4-1 pattern is acceptable. Swashbucklers have been known to use it when 4-4-3-2.

The convention has maximum benefit when the partner of the **CRASH** bidder has 4+ support for at least one suit in each of partner's pairings. This allows a jump reply, which hopefully does maximum damage to the 1♣ opener, who has not yet been able to show a suit. For example,

WEST	NORTH	EAST	SOUTH
1♣	1NT	No	3♣ ...

3♣ is pre-emptive. It shows 4+ clubs and asks partner to pass with clubs and hearts, but to remove to 3◇ if holding diamonds and spades (known as 'Pass-or-Correct'). South will have at least four cards in either diamonds or spades, else the jump to 3♣ would not be safe.

CRASH can also be used for weak two-suited opening bids of 2♡ (Colour), 2♠ (Rank) and 2NT (Shape). See **R.C.O.** on the next page.

R.C.O. If your multi-2$\diamondsuit$ includes a weak two in either major and a strong balanced hand among the options, the 2$\heartsuit$, 2$\spadesuit$ and 2NT openings become free for other purposes. Since a 5-5 or more freakish pattern occurs about as often as a disciplined weak two in a major, you can show a weak two-suiter with these opening bids. **CRASH** is one approach. **RCO** is similar and stands for **R**ank – **C**olour – **O**dd, with 2$\heartsuit$ showing two suits of the same rank, 2$\spadesuit$ same colour, and 2NT the odd suits (spades / diamonds or hearts / clubs: odd because the pairings are of different rank and different colour). A neat way of remembering 2NT is 2NT = 2 **N**on-**T**ouching suits.

RCO was part of the original *Power System* and we used to remember the order of the suits via **R**esponder – **C**an – **O**perate. One of the advantages of **RCO** over **CRASH** is that the major two-suiter is shown more cheaply, 2$\heartsuit$ in **RCO**, 2$\spadesuit$ in **CRASH**. 2$\heartsuit$ may allow a bail-out in 2-Major more easily. Since you have a competitive edge when holding both majors, it does not appeal to give that up by opening 2$\spadesuit$ and pushing the partnership into the three-level more often.

Like **CRASH**, **RCO** can be used against strong 1$\clubsuit$ openings: Double shows **R**ank, 1$\diamondsuit$ is **C**olour and 1NT for **O**dd.

RCO is also effective against 1NT openings since it allows all two-suited combinations to be shown without damaging the single-suited overcalls of 2$\heartsuit$ or 2$\spadesuit$. Over their 1NT, 2$\clubsuit$ = **R**ank, 2$\diamondsuit$ = **C**olour, and against a weak 1NT, 2NT = **O**dd (retaining Double for penalties) while against a strong 1NT, Double = **O**dd, since the opportunities for penalising a strong 1NT are so rare.

Sadly, administrators in many countries bar **CRASH** and **RCO** as opening bids except in major championships, although either method is usually permitted as a defence against their 1NT or their strong 1$\clubsuit$.

CMOBODOR and FILM

These indicate the takeout bids over an opposing three-level pre-empt. **CMOBODOR** stands for **C**heaper-**M**inor-**O**ver-**B**lack (3$\diamondsuit$ over 3$\clubsuit$, and 4$\clubsuit$ over 3$\spadesuit$) **O**ptional-**D**ouble-**O**ver-**R**ed (Double for takeout over 3$\diamondsuit$ or 3$\heartsuit$ openings). **FILM** comes from **FI**shbein – **L**ower **M**inor in which Fishbein is played over a red suit pre-empt (next suit up for takeout, 3$\heartsuit$ over 3$\diamondsuit$, and 3$\spadesuit$ over 3$\heartsuit$) and next minor for takeout applies after a 3$\clubsuit$ or 3$\spadesuit$ opening. Both methods have almost disappeared. Top players usually prefer double for takeout after pre-empts (see **ATP DAFT**: **A**re **T**he **P**oliticians **D**oing **A**nything **F**or **T**axpayers, pages 53-57).

D.A.B. = Directional **A**sking **B**id

This is a bid of the enemy suit to ask partner to bid no-trumps with Q-x or J-x-x (half-stoppers) or stronger holdings in their suit. The partnership needs to specify when a bid of the enemy suit qualifies as a **DAB**.

WEST	NORTH	EAST	SOUTH
1♠	Double	No	2♠ . . .

2♠ here is generally played merely as any strong hand with game prospects but no clear-cut game bid. Over North's reply, 3♠ by South would ask for some stopper in the enemy suit. The prevalent style among top players is that if only one suit has been bid by the opposition, a bid of their suit *asks* for a full stopper (ace, K-x, Q-x-x, J-x-x-x or better). If the opponents have bid or shown two suits, bidding their suit *shows* a stopper in the suit bid and asks partner to bid no-trumps with a full stopper in their other suit.

A half-stopper can be very valuable in no-trumps. With Q-x opposite A-x-x or K-x-x, it is almost always better for the player with Q-x to be the declarer. A repeat bid of the enemy suit can be harnessed to ask for half a stopper. For example,

WEST	NORTH	EAST	SOUTH
1♣	No	1♢	1♠
No	No	2♠	No
3♣	No	3♠ . . .	

2♠ showed a powerful hand and asked for a full stopper in spades. 3♠ now asks for a half-stopper. Perhaps East has a hand such as:

♠ J 4 3   ♡ K 5   ♢ A K Q J 8 7   ♣ 9 5

RKCB = Roman **K**ey-**C**ard **B**lackwood

This is a very effective method of locating aces and the top trump honours for small slams and grand slams. The key cards are the four aces and the king of trumps (the agreed suit or the last bid suit if no suit has been specifically agreed). In reply to 4NT:

5♣ = 0 or 3 key cards
5♢ = 1 or 4 key cards
5♡ = 2 or 5 key cards, no trump queen
5♠ = 2 or 5 key cards plus the trump queen

Some partnerships interchange the 5♣ and 5♢ bids and remember it as **1430** (5♣ = 1 or 4, 5♢ = 3 or 0) as the score for 6♡ or 6♠ vulnerable.

16

DOPI and **DEPO** apply when an opponent bids over 4NT Blackwood and so interferes with the normal ace-showing reply. They can be used whether Simple Blackwood or Roman Key-Card Blackwood is played. **DOPI** stands for **D**ouble = **0**, **P**ass = **1** and the cheapest bid shows 2. **DEPO** is **D**ouble = **E**ven, **P**ass = **O**dd so that Double shows 0, 2 or 4 aces, while Pass shows 1 or 3. **PODI** and **DOPE** are merely the reverse meaning of these. **DOPI** is the most commonly played. It matters little which of these you use as long as both you and partner remember it on the odd occasion when such interference occurs.

When 4NT is doubled, some play **ROPI** (**R**edouble = **0**, **P**ass = **1**, with 5♣ showing 2, and so on), or the reverse, **RIPO**. Most prefer to give the normal reply and ignore the double, as this minimises the risk of any misunderstanding in a situation which occurs very rarely.

SPLASH and TRASH

These are defences over their 1NT opening. **SPLASH** stands for the **S**uit bid **PL**us **A** **S**uit **H**igher. Thus (1NT) : 2♢ shows diamonds plus a major while (1NT): 2♡ shows both majors.

If playing **TRASH**, a suit bid operates either as a transfer or shows the other two suits, **TRA**nsfer or **S**uits **H**igher. For example, (1NT) : 2♣ is either a transfer to diamonds or has both majors, while (1NT) : 2♢ is a transfer to hearts or has both black suits. Partner assumes it is a transfer until proven otherwise.

WEST	NORTH	EAST	SOUTH
1NT	2♢	No	2♡
No	2♠ . . .		

North is now showing the black suits. A bid of 3♣ or 3♢ by North instead of 2♠ would confirm the transfer and show hearts plus the minor suit bid. Some pairs play transfers over 1NT but with (1NT) : 2♣ as the only **TRASH** overcall (diamonds or both majors). Personally, as long as the partnership can handle it, I prefer playing **RCO** over 1NT.

EHAA and KISS

These are two of my favourites. **E**very **H**and **A**n **A**dventure is a roller-coaster ride featuring undisciplined weak twos in all suits, a mini-1NT opening (10-12), 4-card majors and heavy pre-emption when a good fit is found. **K**eep **I**t **S**imple, **S**tupid is good advice for any partnership and any system. *If you give partner a chance to err, partner grabs the chance.*

2♡ : 2NT and 2♠ : 2NT – The Ogust Convention

The 2NT reply to a weak two shows strength and asks whether the opening is minimum (6-8 HCP) or maximum (9-10 HCP) and how many of the top three honours are held in opener's major. The replies are:

3♣ = minimum, **1** top honour
3♢ = minimum, **2** top honours
3♡ = maximum, **1** top honour
3♠ = maximum, **2** top honours
3NT = all **3** honours, A-K-Q-x-x-x and obviously little else

A simple way to remember all of this is to picture **Mama Mimi** dancing, **one – two, one – two – three** . . . The numbers refer to the order in which the top honours in the major are shown and **Mama Mimi** stems from **MA**jors **MA**ximum, **MI**nors **MI**nimum, **1-2**, **1-2-3**.

Another useful reminder is **RONF** if you play change of suit is forcing after a weak two. **RONF** stands for **R**aise **O**nly **N**on-**F**orce

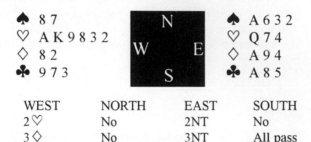

♠ 8 7
♡ A K 9 8 3 2
♢ 8 2
♣ 9 7 3

♠ A 6 3 2
♡ Q 7 4
♢ A 9 4
♣ A 8 5

WEST	NORTH	EAST	SOUTH
2♡	No	2NT	No
3♢	No	3NT	All pass

One of the strengths of 2NT Ogust is the ability to determine when 3NT is likely to be a better spot than the major suit contract. When West bids 3♢ to show a minimum with two top honours in hearts, East can place West with ♡A-K-x-x-x-x. As that is 7 HCP, West cannot hold more than an extra jack. That means that there are only nine tricks available in hearts. With instant winners and every suit covered, East can see that the same nine tricks are available in no-trumps.

3NT is an excellent chance. As East you will naturally take the cost-nothing precaution of starting the hearts by playing the queen first to guard against South holding ♡J-10-6-5.

Lebensohl after interference over your 1NT

WEST	NORTH	EAST	SOUTH
1NT	2♠	?	

When playing Lebensohl, a new suit at the three-level is forcing to game, while a bid of 2NT forces opener to bid 3♣. A new suit then by responder is to play. Responder can also show a strong hand by bidding the enemy suit or 3NT, either directly or after the 2NT puppet to 3♣.

W	N	E	S	W	N	E	S
1NT	2♠	3♠ . . .		1NT	2♠	2NT	No
3♠ = Stayman with no stopper in spades				3♣	No	3♠ . . .	
				3♠ = Stayman + stopper in spades			
W	N	E	S	W	N	E	S
1NT	2♠	3NT . . .		1NT	2♠	2NT	No
3NT = no spade stopper				3♣	No	3NT . . .	
				3NT = stopper in spades			

How are you supposed to remember which way round these bids go? An easy alliteration indicates whether responder holds a stopper in their suit: **SLOW SHOWS, DIRECT DENIES**. This means that if you bid 3NT directly or bid their suit (as Stayman) directly, you deny a stopper in their suit (**Direct Denies**). If you take the slow, long route (via the 2NT puppet to 3♣), you are showing a stopper in their suit (**Slow Shows**).

UDAC: This excellent system of signalling stands for <u>U</u>pside <u>D</u>own <u>A</u>ttitude and <u>C</u>ount, also known as 'reverse signals'.

For <u>U</u>pside <u>D</u>own <u>A</u>tttitude: To encourage partner to continue a suit, play your lowest; to discourage the suit led and ask for a shift, play the highest you can afford. This is superior to high-encourage since you may not always be able to afford a high card but you can always afford your lowest. If you hate the suit, you can surely afford to play high.

For <u>U</u>pside <u>D</u>own <u>C</u>ount: Lowest card shows an even number of cards. High-Then-Low shows an odd number. Again the theory is that you may not be able to afford the highest card from a doubleton, while the lowest cannot be a problem. From three cards, if you cannot afford the highest, you can still play middle followed by the lowest to show an odd number.

How do you remember this, especially if you have been playing high-encourage for so many years? Easy: **LOW LIKES, HIGH HATES**

CHAPTER 3

10 LITTLE TRIGGERS FOR BIDDING

1. The Basketball Players' Rule

(a) What action do you take as dealer with:

♠ 4 2   ♡ 8 3   ◇ K Q 6 4   ♣ A K 7 3 2

(b) What action do you take as dealer with:

♠ A Q 8 7 3   ♡ 6   ◇ 8   ♣ A Q 8 6 5 2

(c) Partner opens 1♣. What is your response with:

♠ J 3   ♡ K 8 7 5   ◇ Q J 6 3 2   ♣ 7 4

(d) Partner opens 1 ◇. What is your response with:

♠ A Q 7 6   ♡ 7 5   ◇ J 6   ♣ K Q 9 6 2

None of these poses a problem if you follow the **Basketball Players' Rule**: **Longest First**. That means 1♣ on (a) and (b), 1 ◇ on (c) and 2♣ on (d).

Some wish to open 1 ◇ with (a) and rebid 2♣. This runs the risk of receiving preference to diamonds when responder has equal length in the minors and thus playing in the inferior trump fit. Recommended is to open 1♣ and rebid 2♣ over a major suit response.

With (b), opening 1♠ is a common fault for some, particularly if they play 5-card majors. After this opening, partner can never be convinced you hold so many clubs and the best contract might be in clubs, even 6♣ or 7♣. Best is to open 1♣, then bid and rebid spades. See Trigger 2.

With (c), some like to bypass diamonds and bid the major first. This can cause you to miss a diamond part-score. If you bid 1 ◇, longest first, you will find any diamond contract and allow opener to rebid in hearts and become declarer in a heart contract. If an opponent intervenes in spades, a double for takeout by either partner can locate a fit in hearts.

If you bid spades first with (d), then the length in clubs cannot be shown later. Bid 2♣ first and rebid in spades over 2 ◇ or 2NT. Choose a 1♠ response with such shape only if not strong enough for a 2♣ reply.

2. ABB and ABA

What is your plan of bidding with each of these hands as dealer, assuming partner responds 2♣ or 2♢?

(a) ♠ K J 4 3 2 ♡ K J 9 7 2 ♢ 7 2 ♣ A	(b) ♠ K J 9 6 3 ♡ K Q 6 4 3 2 ♢ 2 ♣ A	(c) ♠ K J 9 6 3 2 ♡ K Q 4 3 ♢ 7 2 ♣ A

ABB and **ABA** are reminders of how to show hand patterns. **ABB** stands for 1st suit, 2nd suit, repeat 2nd suit and applies when showing a 5-5 or a 6-5 pattern. With Hand (a), you open 1♠ and over 2♣ or 2♢, rebid 2♡. If partner then continues with 2NT, rebid 3♡. Repeating the hearts shows a 5-card suit and therefore 3♡ shows at least 5-5 in the majors.

With Hand (b), open 1♡ *(the basketball players' rule)*. Over 2♣ or 2♢, rebid 2♠. Your HCP are below expectancy for a reverse, but your playing strength justifies bidding beyond your 2♡ 'barrier'. A reverse usually has 16+ HCP and five losers or fewer. With only four losers, you can bid 2♠ without qualms. If partner continues with 2NT or 3-minor, rebid 3♠ (**ABB**). Rebidding the suit shows five spades and hence six or more hearts for the 1♡ opening. Having disclosed eleven of your thirteen cards to partner, you will accept partner's decision as to the contract.

ABA is 1st suit, 2nd suit, 1st suit again, the order of showing suits with a 6-4 pattern (provided that you do not mislead partner as to your strength when you show your 4-card suit). With Hand (c), open 1♠ and over 2♣ or 2♢, rebid 2♡. If partner continues with 2NT, rebid 3♠. The 2♡ rebid showed 5-4 in the majors and 3♠ now shows the extra card in spades.

♠ 9 ♡ K J 5 2 ♢ J 8 ♣ A K 7 4 3 2	With this 6-4, open 1♣ and rebid 1♡ over a 1♢ response. Then rebid the clubs after a 1NT or 2NT rebid from partner. However, after 1♣ : 1♠, you are not good enough for 2♡ and will have to settle for a 2♣ rebid to show a minimum opening.

♠ A K Q 9 7 ♡ 8 7 6 5 3 2 ♢ A 4 ♣ - - -	The rules are not written in stone. If there is a great disparity in suit strengths, you may elect to bid in the suits in 'abnormal' order. With the hand on the left, it is sensible to open 1♠ and bid hearts next as though you had a 5-5 pattern.

3. 'With 6-4, Bid More' and 'With 6-5, Come Alive'

Point count generally fails to estimate the playing strength accurately when the hands are very shapely. Take a look at these:

A. ♠ K Q 9 8 3 2 ♥ 8 ♦ K 10 3 ♣ 6 4 2	B. ♠ K Q 9 8 3 2 ♥ 8 ♦ K 10 4 3 ♣ 6 4	C. ♠ K Q 9 8 3 2 ♥ 8 ♦ K 10 9 4 3 ♣ 6

Each hand has 8 HCP but Hand A has 7 losers, Hand B has 6 losers and Hand C has only 5. Hand A is a maximum weak 2♠ opening. Weak twos usually have 7-8 losers. Hand B also qualifies as a weak 2♠, but with the extra playing trick, you are unlikely to do damage if you open this 3♠, particularly if not vulnerable. The 3♠ opening does far more damage to the opponents than 2♠ especially as there is so little room for them to manoeuvre between your 3♠ and the possibility of 3NT as their contract.

This deal from a 1998 national championship highlights the playing strength of the 6-4:

Dealer South : East-West vulnerable

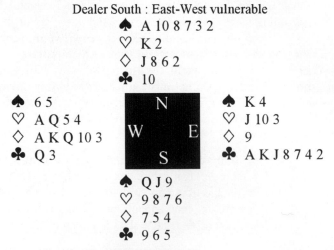

```
              ♠ A 10 8 7 3 2
              ♡ K 2
              ♢ J 8 6 2
              ♣ 10

   ♠ 6 5                        ♠ K 4
   ♡ A Q 5 4      N             ♡ J 10 3
   ♢ A K Q 10 3  W   E          ♢ 9
   ♣ Q 3            S           ♣ A K J 8 7 4 2

              ♠ Q J 9
              ♡ 9 8 7 6
              ♢ 7 5 4
              ♣ 9 6 5
```

With 6♣ or 6NT available for East-West, the datum (average) was only +790 to E-W. The damage to slam prospects often resulted from a jump to 3♠ by North over West's 1♦. Fear of penalties is often an inhibiting factor but the vulnerability should ease any anxiety in bidding 3♠. Even if doubled, 3♠ costs a mere 300 on the actual layout. What a bargain.

If bidding up with a **6-4** is good value, it must be more so with wilder shape. Eddie Kantar's **'With 6-5, Come Alive'** urges you to do something with a freakish hand. You must not pass with Hand C on the previous page. If the spades were stronger, opening 4♣ is sensible. If not prepared to do that, open 1♠. Do not pass. Come alive. With five losers, the playing strength is much too good for a 2♠ or 3♠ opening (wash out my mouth with soap for even suggesting either of these).

Here is an example from the same national championship:

Dealer South : North-South vulnerable

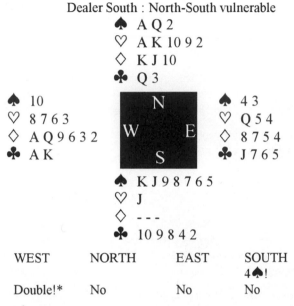

```
                    ♠ A Q 2
                    ♡ A K 10 9 2
                    ◇ K J 10
                    ♣ Q 3
      ♠ 10                         ♠ 4 3
      ♡ 8 7 6 3          N         ♡ Q 5 4
      ◇ A Q 9 6 3 2   W     E      ◇ 8 7 5 4
      ♣ A K             S          ♣ J 7 6 5
                    ♠ K J 9 8 7 6 5
                    ♡ J
                    ◇ - - -
                    ♣ 10 9 8 4 2
```

WEST	NORTH	EAST	SOUTH
			4♠!
Double!*	No	No	No

*For takeout

No one could accuse South of cowardice. With 7-5, *he* came alive. 4♠ doubled made with an overtrick for +990. Do not blame West for the outcome: he was following **'With 6-4, Bid More'**. Had East taken the double out, as requested, by bidding 4NT (to show a choice of suits), the contract might have been 5◇ doubled which is only three down, −500.

Examples such as these are not isolated instances. You will not come up smelling of roses every time you take strong action on freakish shapes but you will experience a preponderance of happiness over misery, and isn't that a basic aim of life? So, bid more and come alive.

4. The Rule of 3 and 2

With neither side vulnerable, what would you do as dealer with these?

A. ♠ A K Q 10 6 5 3	B. ♠ - - -
♡ 8	♡ 6 3
♢ 8 5 4	♢ A Q J 8 7 6 4 3 2
♣ 9 6	♣ 8 7

There are players who will pre-empt to the three-level but never any higher. Such players would open 3♠ on Hand A and 3♢ with Hand B. Such actions suffer from two defects: they fail to exert maximum pressure on the opponents and they do not give partner an accurate description of your playing strength.

The Rule of 3 and 2 states that with a weak hand (up to 10 HCP) and a long, strong suit, you should count your playing tricks and **add 3** *when not vulnerable*, **add 2** *if vulnerable*. Then bid for that number of tricks.

Counting losers is a sound way to estimate playing tricks. A singleton is 1 loser (except for singleton ace), a doubleton is two losers (except for A-K, no losers, or A-x or K-x, 1 loser each) and for a suit of three cards or longer, the ace, king and queen are the critical cards. Count one loser for each of these top cards missing, with a maximum of 3 losers per suit.

Hand A has 6 losers (0 in spades, 1 in hearts, 3 in diamonds and 2 in clubs). 13 cards – 6 losers = 7 playing tricks. Not vulnerable, adding 3 = 10 and so you should open for ten tricks, 4♠. To open 3♠ is like opening 1NT, 12-14, when you have 17 points. You are underbidding your cards.

It is clearly harder for the opponents to bid over 4♠ than over 3♠. If you open 3♠, partner places you with 6 playing tricks and may pass when game is on, or raise to 4♠ when slam is on. When you open 4♠, partner places you with 7 playing tricks and should be able to estimate the combined potential more accurately.

Similarly, Hand B has five losers and therefore eight playing tricks. Adding on 3 not vulnerable takes you to 11. Therefore, open 5♢.

Some daredevils follow the Rule of 2, 3, 4 or 5 for pre-empts: 2 short at unfavourable vulnerability, 3 short when both vulnerable, up to 4 short if neither side is vulnerable and up to 5 short at favourable. They may not always win but I bet they have a lot of fun.

5. The Rule of 15 for opening the bidding in fourth seat

The bidding goes No Bid, No Bid, No Bid to you. What action would you take with each of these hands?

A. ♠ K Q 6 5	B. ♠ 9 8	C. ♠ A K J 10 4
♡ 9 8	♡ K Q 6 5	♡ 8 2
◇ 6 2	◇ 6 2	◇ Q 10 9 3
♣ A Q 5 3 2	♣ A Q 5 3 2	♣ 6 2

When there are three passes to you, make your normal opening bid with 13 HCP or more. If you have 13, there are 27 HCP missing and partner's fair share is 9, giving your side the balance of power. The real question is whether to open with a hand in the 9-12 HCP range. The **Rule of 15** provides guidelines to answer this question.

In fourth seat, add the number of spades held to your HCP.

If the total is 15 or more, make your normal opening bid.

If the total is below 15, pass the hand in.

When you have below 13 points, chances are that the points are evenly divided between the two sides. If so, the side that owns the spade suit is likely to win the part-score battle. If you open in fourth seat and they bid up to 2♠, you either have to sell out (and they are likely to succeed) or bid to the three-level where you will probably fail. In either case you go minus when you could simply pass the hand in. By contrast, if you own the spade suit, you figure to win the part-score.

According to the **Rule of 15**, you open 1♣ on Hand A and No Bid with Hand B. Playing weak twos, opening 2♠ on Hand C is best, otherwise 1♠.

6. A powerful bridge hand is like a great love affair

WEST	NORTH	EAST	SOUTH
2♣	No	2◇	No
?			

What action would you take as West with these cards:

♠ A K Q J 10 8
♡ A K Q
◇ A 7
♣ A 2

There are some who might ask for aces in order to ask for kings next and curse their bad luck when partner has none. Others might jump to 3♠ to set the trump suit irrevocably, asking partner to cue-bid with an ace and bid 3NT with no aces but at least one king. Neither of these would come close to finding the grand slam on these cards.

♠ A K Q J 10 8		♠ 3
♥ A K Q	N	♥ J 10 7 6 3 2
◇ A 7	W E	◇ 6 3 2
♣ A 2	S	♣ 9 5 3

Eleven tricks is the limit in spades or no-trumps but 7♥ should be easy. Remember the 'love affair' rule and you can handle such problems.

A powerful bridge hand is like a great love affair. Don't rush it.

After 2♣ : 2◇, a simple 2♠ rebid, forcing to game, will achieve it all.

WEST	NORTH	EAST	SOUTH
2♣	No	2◇	No
2♠	No	3♥	No
7♥	No	No	No

East's 3♥ promises no extra points but a 5+ heart suit. That is enough for West. In the worst scenario, 7♥ will require a 3-2 split in hearts.

7. Defend on odd occasions

This maxim advises against competing for a part-score above the opponents at the three-level (three being an odd number) and against competing over their five-level contract (five being an odd number).

The advice is sound but there are many factors which can reasonably influence you to bid on nevertheless. The rule is sensible because it focuses attention on the basic stance to adopt. To act contrary to the maxim you should have some powerful reason(s).

At the part-score level, the 3-over-3 rule is more helpful (see Trigger 8). At the five-level, the decision to bid above them may be influenced by the loser count, freakish shape, a void in their suit (usually worth an extra trick in offence) or a lack of defence against their contract.

8. The 3-over-2, 3-over-3 and 4-over-3 Rules

These offer guide-lines about competing for a part-score when a known trump fit exists.

3-over-2: If the opponents bid and raise a suit to the two-level and there are two passes to you, it is almost always right to compete.

WEST	NORTH	EAST	SOUTH
1♠	2♦	2♠	No
No	?		

North should almost never sell out to 2♠. As the opponents have stopped at two, the points are roughly even between the two sides. In that case, each side can usually make eight tricks in its trump fit. To pass is give East-West an easy run. North's task is to drive East-West from the safety of the two-level to the jeopardy of the three-level. You must be prepared to risk the three-level yourself, and possibly fail there, to achieve this result. Usually the best way for North to compete is with a takeout double.

Despite this advice, you may choose to defend at the two-level if the opponents are notorious underbidders, if West tranced for some time before passing 2♠ or if you have a strong holding in their suit.

3-over-3: Once the bidding has reached the three-level and there is no prospect for game, choose to defend unless your side is known to hold at least nine trumps. With eight trumps, pass and defend. With nine trumps, bid three over their three.

WEST	NORTH	EAST	SOUTH
1♠	2♥	2♠	3♥
No	No	?	

East should pass unless sure that a 9-card trump fit is held.

4-over-3: If the values indicate no more than a part-score, do not compete to the four-level against their three-level contract. Mostly you will fail when they might fail, and at the four-level they start doubling.

The rules can be summarised as follows:

3-over-2 : ✓	3-over-3 : ?	4-over-3 : X
Almost always	Maybe	Almost never

9. Type A, Type B and Type C Takeout Doubles

Takeout doubles cover a lot of territory and so require considerable learning. It is easy to remember the requirements and strategies involved by breaking the takeout double into smaller components (known as 'chunking' in memory psychology). These rules operate when an opponent has opened and you wish to double for takeout.

Type A:

Range: *12-15 HCP.* Can be less with classical shape (4-4-4-1 or 5-4-4-0 with the shortage in the enemy suit — see Rule of 15, Part 2, page 38).

Hand Type: 1. *Shortest suit must be the enemy suit*
               2. *Must have 3+ cards in any unbid suit*

Strategy: Double and then pass any minimum reply from partner. The Type A double typically has 6-7 losers.

Type B:

Range: *16-18 HCP.*

Hand Type: *Any type other than one suitable for a 1NT overcall.* The hand may not fit 1NT because it is not balanced, because it has a 5-card major or because it has no stopper in the enemy suit.

If the hand fits 1NT, choose that. *Exception:* If their opening is 1♣ or 1◇ and you have a 4-4-3-2 pattern with both majors, 16-18 points and their suit stopped, double is preferable to 1NT since the odds are very good that your side has a major suit fit.

Strategy: Double and then bid again without a jump-bid. The doubler may raise partner or bid a new suit. Double + raise *or* double + bid is the sign of a Type B double which usually has 5 losers but can have 6 losers if the hand is balanced.

Type C:

Range: *19+ HCP.*

Hand Type: *Any.*

Strategy: Double and then bid again with a jump-bid or in no-trumps or by bidding the enemy suit. The doubler's next action clarifies further:

Double + no-trumps at cheapest level: 19-21 balanced, stopper in their suit

Double + jump-rebid to 2NT: 22-23 balanced, stopper in their suit

Double + jump-raise or jump new suit: 4 losers, needs one trick for game

Double + bid enemy suit: 19+ and unsure of direction *or* enough for game but not sure of the best game.

Right-hand opponent opens 1♦. You double and partner bids 1♠. Classify your double into Type A, Type B or Type C and decide on your next action.

a. ♠ K 6	b. ♠ Q J 7 2	c. ♠ A J 5
♥ A Q 9	♥ K Q 9	♥ K 7 2
♦ 8 5	♦ 4 2	♦ 9 7 4
♣ A K Q 7 6 4	♣ A 9 7 3	♣ A K J 2
d. ♠ A K 6 5	e. ♠ A 10 7 3	f. ♠ K Q 3
♥ K Q 8 3	♥ K Q J 4	♥ A K J 4
♦ 8	♦ 2	♦ K 9 5 2
♣ K J 6 4	♣ A K Q 2	♣ A 6

a. Type C. Double and jump to 3♣ (not forcing) to show the 4-loser hand.
b. Type A. Double and pass 1♠.
c. Type B. Double and pass 1♠. Normally you make a second bid with Type B but with 7-8 losers, game is most unlikely if partner was unable to make a jump-reply to the double.
d. Type B. Double and raise to 2♠ to show the 5-loser hand.
e. Type C. Double and jump-raise to 3♠ to show 4 losers.
f. Type C. Double and rebid 1NT to show 19-21 balanced with at least one stopper in their suit.

10. The MAFIA Principle

WEST	NORTH	EAST	SOUTH
1♣	Double	No	?

What should South do with these hands?

a. ♠ 9 8 6 5	b. ♠ 5	c. ♠ J 8 4 3
♥ 5 2	♥ J 7 4 3	♥ Q 2
♦ A K J 5	♦ Q 9 8 4 2	♦ A K 9 4 3
♣ 8 7 4	♣ 8 6 4	♣ 6 2

MAFIA stands for **MA**jors **FI**rst **A**lways *in reply to a takeout double* (even with a stronger or longer minor). To reply in a minor suit denies a 4+ major. MAFIA means the doubler need not worry that a 4-4 major suit fit has been missed if advancer (partner of the doubler) replies in a minor suit. Therefore the answers to the questions are: a. 1♠ b. 1♥ c. 2♠.

CHAPTER 4

10 LITTLE TRIGGERS FOR CARD PLAY

1. The Rule of 11

The benefits stemming from the **Rule of 11** are few and far between but you have to use it hand after hand so that you do not miss out when a gain does occur. The rule applies when the opening lead is fourth highest and states:

Deduct the pips on the card led from 11.

The answer is the number of higher cards (than the one led) in the other three hands.

The rule can benefit both declarer and the third hand defender.

NORTH *(Dummy)*

A Q 8

EAST *(You)*

K 9 3

South has opened 1NT, passed out. West leads the 6, the 8 is played from dummy. Your move?

Rule of 11 to the rescue. Deduct the lead (6) from 11. Answer: 5. That means there are five cards higher than the 6 in dummy, your hand and declarer's. Dummy has three of these cards, you have two. Therefore declarer cannot beat the 6. Thus you can tell that playing the 9 will win the trick. The full layout is:

A Q 8

J 10 7 6   K 9 3

5 4 2

If you play the king, declarer has two tricks. Play the 9 and you restrict declarer to one.

NORTH	West leads the 7. How should you play?
A 9 3	If the lead is 4th highest, the **Rule of 11** applies. 7 from 11
	= 4. As you can see 4 cards higher than the 7, East has 0.
SOUTH	Play dummy's 9. That gives you three tricks if West has
Q J 2	led from K-10-8-7-(x). Play the 3 and you make just two.

2. The Rule of 12

1.	NORTH	2.	NORTH	3.	NORTH
	Q 10 3 2		J 7		Q 9 2
	SOUTH		SOUTH		SOUTH
	A J 6 4		A Q 10 5 4 3		A J 10 4 3

One hand has a tenace missing the king. The opposite hand holds one or more cards equal in rank to the lower card(s) in the tenace. In #1, the A-J is the tenace and the Q-10 opposite are equal in rank to the jack, the lower card of the tenace. Given you intend to finesse for the king, how should you handle these combinations, assuming you have plenty of entries to North?

The question is whether you should lead low from North to finesse or whether you can you afford to lead a high card from dummy and let it run. The **Rule of 12** provides the answer: *With 8, 9 or 10 cards in the two hands, if the number of cards in the two hands plus the cards in sequence totals 12 or more, you can afford to lead a high card opposite the tenace and let it run. If the total is below 12, lead low to the tenace.*

In #1 you have 8 cards and 3 cards (Q, J and 10) in sequence. 8 + 3 = 11, and so it is not safe to lead the Q or 10 from North. The right play is low from North to the jack in hand. If the jack wins, return to North and then lead the queen or ten to repeat the finesse. The layout could be:

```
                 Q 10 3 2
     9 8 7 5                  K
                 A J 6 4
```

Lead the queen or ten on the first round and you lose a trick. Start with a low card from North and you have all the tricks. If entries to the North hand are a problem, take the risk and lead an honour from North.

The answer for #2 is the same: 8 cards + 3 in sequence. Therefore it is not safe to lead the jack on the first round. Again, king singleton would cost you a trick. As long as entries to North are comfortable, start by leading the 7 to your 10. If that wins, return to dummy and lead the jack for the second finesse.

In #3, you have 8 cards + 4 in sequence. It is therefore safe to lead the queen or the 9 for the first-round finesse. Even a singleton king onside does you no harm.

4.	NORTH A Q 7 6 SOUTH J 5 4 3 2	5.	NORTH J 10 2 SOUTH A Q 7 6 5 4	6.	NORTH Q 2 SOUTH A J 7 6 5 4 3

In #4, 9 cards + 2 in sequence (Q and J) = 11. The **Rule of 12** tells you that you should lead low on the first round, not the jack. Play low to the queen. If that wins, cash the ace. To lead the jack first would cost a trick if the king is singleton in this position:

$$A Q 7 6$$
$$K \qquad\qquad 10\ 9\ 8$$
$$J 5\ 4\ 3\ 2$$

#5: 9 cards + 3 in sequence: Total 12. Therefore it is safe to lead the jack or ten first.

#6: 9 cards + 2 in sequence: Total 11. It is not safe to lead the queen first. If East has king singleton, playing the queen costs you a trick while leading the 2 from North avoids losing a trick.

7.	J 8 7 6 4 A Q 5 3 2	#7: 10 + 2 = 12. It is safe to lead the jack. In fact, it makes no difference whether you start with the jack or lead low to the queen first.

8.	J 7 6 4 2 A Q 9 3 2	This time you *should* lead the jack first. If East started with K-10-8, low to the queen leaves you with a loser but jack first can avoid losing a trick.

The **Rule of 12** also applies when missing the king *and* queen, as here:

9.	NORTH 10 9 5 2 SOUTH A J 6 4	10.	NORTH 10 7 SOUTH A J 9 5 4 3	11.	NORTH 9 4 2 SOUTH A J 10 6 5 3

#9 and #10: 8 cards + 3 in sequence = 11. Therefore, do not lead a high card on the first round. Start with a low card from North. To lead high from North costs a trick if East has a singleton honour. You can lead high from North for the second round finesse.

#11: 9 cards + 3 in sequence: It is safe to start with the 9 from North.

3. The Rule of 7

This rule is used by declarer in no-trumps to decide how often to hold up an ace from A-x-x opposite x-x or x-x-x. The idea is to exhaust third hand of the suit led when the opening lead is from a 5-card suit.

Deduct from 7 the number of cards held by you and dummy.

The answer tells you how often to hold up. With A-x-x opposite x-x-x, you have six cards. 7 minus 6 = 1, so hold up once only. With A-x-x opposite x-x, 7 minus 5 = 2, so hold up twice. On any given hand, there may be other considerations but the **Rule of 7** is a good starting point. At pairs, the quest for overtricks may over-ride the **Rule of 7**.

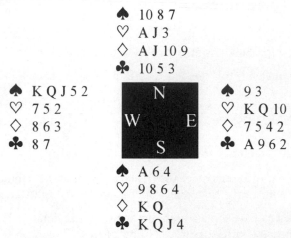

Against 3NT, West leads the king of spades and continues with the queen of spades if South holds off. How often should South hold up the ace?

The **Rule of 7** says 'Hold up once' as declarer + dummy have six cards and 7 minus 6 = 1. South takes the second round of spades, knocks out the ace of clubs and has nine tricks. If East has a spade to return, the spades were originally 4-3 and declarer still loses just four tricks.

If South wins the first trick, a spade return by East after taking the ♣A gives the defence five tricks.

If South errs and holds off twice, West may well shift to hearts at trick 3, setting up two heart tricks for East who still has the ♣A. A heart shift at trick 2 would give the defence only four tricks.

4. Odd numbers break evenly, even numbers break oddly

This refers to the most probable split of the missing cards in any suit.

If you are missing an odd number of cards, chances are that they will divide as evenly as possible between the two opponents.

7 cards missing: probable division 4-3 (c. 60%)

5 cards missing: probable division 3-2 (c. 70%)

3 cards missing: probable division 2-1 (c. 80%)

If you are missing an even number of cards, chances are that they will not divide evenly between the two opponents.

8 cards missing: probable division 5-3 (c. 50%); 4-4 split about 30%.

6 cards missing: probable division 4-2 (c. 50%); 3-3 split about 35%.

4 cards missing: probable division 3-1 (c. 50%); 2-2 split about 40%.

The exception is when 2 cards are missing. The 1-1 split is 52% while the 2-0 break is 48%.

5. An easy way to remember the common breaks

There is a simple way to remember the frequency of the most common divisions of the enemy cards. Note that it applies only to the splits given.

Most of the time you have eight trumps between you and dummy. How often will the opponents' cards divide 3-2? How often 4-1?

To find the answer, simply reverse the numbers. The 3-2 break occurs about 2/3 of the time, the 4-1 split about 1/4 of the time. These answers are correct within about 3% and are certainly good enough for practical purposes. If the choice for success is between taking a finesse, 50%, or relying on a 3-2 break, the 3-2 break is the better bet. It also means that you are not the unluckiest player in the country if you suffer a 4-1 break. Indeed, you can expect about three 4-1 breaks during a normal session.

With a 7-card suit, the 4-2 split of the 6 cards missing occurs 2/4 or half the time. The 3-3 split is not 100% but only around 35%. That is why an 8-card trump suit is attractive (the favourable split is a 2/3 chance) and the 7-card trump suit is risky (the bad break is the 2/3 chance).

6. Use a queen to wake partner up

When partner leads the ace from ace-king, signal with the queen from a Q-J sequence. The queen is from Q-J or Q-singleton and tells partner that you can win the next round of the suit if partner plays low next.

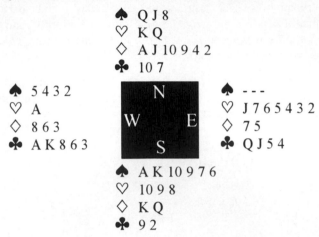

```
              ♠ Q J 8
              ♡ K Q
              ◇ A J 10 9 4 2
              ♣ 10 7
♠ 5 4 3 2                      ♠ - - -
♡ A                            ♡ J 7 6 5 4 3 2
◇ 8 6 3            N           ◇ 7 5
♣ A K 8 6 3   W       E        ♣ Q J 5 4
                   S
              ♠ A K 10 9 7 6
              ♡ 10 9 8
              ◇ K Q
              ♣ 9 2
```

South is in 4♠ and has plenty of tricks. The defence needs to take the first four tricks, impossible if West starts by cashing the top clubs. On the ♣A lead, East signals with ♣Q. West then cashes ♡A, leads a low club to East's jack and the heart ruff defeats 4♠.

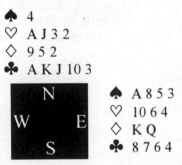

```
              ♠ 4
              ♡ A J 3 2
              ◇ 9 5 2
              ♣ A K J 10 3
                   N          ♠ A 8 5 3
              W       E       ♡ 10 6 4
                   S          ◇ K Q
                              ♣ 8 7 6 4
```

South is in 4♡ after opening 1♡. West leads the ♠J to East's ace. How should East continue?

If you play ◇K, then ◇Q, West with ◇A-8-4-3 might duck. Play ◇Q, then ◇K to alert partner to overtake and give you a diamond ruff.

7. Red-on-black, black-on-red to wake partner up

When giving a signal in discarding, provided that you can afford it, discard from the suit of the opposite colour to the suit led. That increases the chance that partner will take note of the card you are playing. If declarer is drawing trumps in a spade contract and you discard a club, partner may not notice it at all. Following the play only haphazardly, partner may think you are following to the trump. Playing the opposite colour should jolt partner back to concentration.

The corollary is *red-on-red, black-on-black*: 'If you wish declarer to miscount while drawing trumps, discard from the suit of the same colour as the trump suit.' A sleepy declarer may miss it and your reward comes later when declarer says, 'I was sure all the trumps had gone.'

8. K.L.W.D. — Keep Lighthouse Wick Dry

```
              Dummy
              A Q 6 4
WEST                    EAST
J 9 8                   7 5 3 2
              SOUTH
              K 10
```

Declarers often lead out a long suit in the hope that the defenders will discard incorrectly. In the above layout, declarer has three winners but if East discards from that apparently worthless holding, declarer has four tricks in the suit. **K.L.W.D.** will stop East from falling into this trap.

K.	Keep	Keep
L.	Length	Lighthouse
W.	With	Wick
D.	Dummy	Dry

Provided you can beat at least one of dummy's cards, do not reduce your length below dummy's. When dummy has five or more cards and you hold four, it pays to retain all your length to minimise the number of tricks declarer can develop from that suit, as long as you can beat at least one of dummy's top four cards.

Similarly, if you know from the bidding that declarer has a 4-card or longer suit, **K.L.W.D.** — Keep – Length – With – Declarer.

9. L.O.E.I.T.S. — London or Edinburgh in the Spring

Average players can sharpen their game by playing the correct card in third seat. A defender wins a trick as cheaply as possible. Similarly, when playing third hand high, play the cheapest of equally high cards.

L.	Lowest	London
O.	Of	Or
E.	Equals	Edinburgh
I.	In	In
T.	Third	The
S.	Seat	Spring

Lead top of sequences, *signal* with top of sequences but in third hand high or when winning a trick, *play the lowest of touching cards.*

1.	NORTH		2.	NORTH		3.	NORTH	
	7 6 4			7 6 4			7 6 4	
		EAST			EAST			EAST
		A K 3			K Q 5			Q J 10 2

If West leads low, #1 East plays the king (denying the queen), #2 East plays the queen (denying the jack) and #3 East plays the 10 (denying the 9). *The card played in third-hand-high denies the next lower card.*

10. R.T.T. — Raise The Titanic

How do you handle these combinations to make maximum tricks?

1.	A J 5 4 2	2.	A Q 5 3	3.	A 9 4 2
	K 8 7 6 3		K 10 6 2		K Q 6 3

With a tenace in one hand and a winner or winners opposite, start with the winner(s) opposite the tenace. In #1, cash the king first (to guard against Q-10-9 with West); in #2, play ace and queen first (caters for J-x-x-x with East); in #3, start with king and queen (avoids a loser if West began with 10-x-x-x or J-x-x-x). R.T.T. expresses the principle: **Retain The Tenace** by cashing the winner(s) opposite the tenace first.

R.	Retain	Raise
T.	The	The
T.	Tenace	Titanic

CHAPTER 5

BIDDING STRATEGY

Rule of 15, Part 1

Suppose right-hand opponent opens 1♠. What do you do with these?

(a) ♠ 8	(b) ♠ 7	(c) ♠ 2
♡ 6 2	♡ 4 2	♡ 4
◇ K Q 10 9 5	◇ A J 7 3 2	◇ Q 10 8 6 5 3
♣ Q J 9 8 4	♣ Q 6 4 3 2	♣ K J 8 4 2

For the Unusual 2NT, not only should you have at least 5-5 in the minors but your long suits should also be strong. How strong?

To the number of cards in the minors add the number of honour cards in the minors. If the answer is 15+, your suits are good enough.

To use this rule, count the 10 or J as an honour only if the suit contains another honour as well. That means you should bid 2NT on (a), which measures 15, pass with (b), total only 13, and bid 2NT with (c), also 15. This **Rule of 15** applies analogously if you play Michaels Cue Bids.

Rule of 15, Part 2

Suppose right-hand opponent opens 1♠. What do you do with these?

(a) ♠ K 6 3	(b) ♠ 5	(c) ♠ - - -
♡ K Q 4 3	♡ A Q 3 2	♡ Q 10 5 2
◇ 8 7 5	◇ K J 7	◇ A 10 7 5 3
♣ A Q 3	♣ J 8 6 4 3	♣ K 7 6 2

Australian international, Seamus Browne, has suggested a useful test to decide whether a hand qualifies for a Type A double (see page 28).

Count your HCP. Add two points for each card below three in the opponent's suit. If the answer is 15 or more, the hand qualifies for a takeout double (assuming that a 1NT overcall or suit overcall is not superior).

In other words, to your HCP add 6 for a void, 4 for a singleton or 2 for a doubleton in the enemy suit. Consider double if the total is 15+. On that basis, No bid with (a), double with (b) and double with (c).

Hand (c) arose in the semi-finals of the 1998 Pacific Asian Teams Championship. This was the complete deal:

Dealer North : Nil vulnerable

```
                    ♠ 10 8 3
                    ♡ K 9 6
                    ◇ J 9 8 4 2
                    ♣ A 4
   ♠ Q J 7 2                        ♠ A K 9 6 5 4
   ♡ A 8 4 3         N              ♡ J 7
   ◇ Q          W         E         ◇ K 6
   ♣ J 10 8 3         S             ♣ Q 9 5
                    ♠ - - -
                    ♡ Q 10 5 2
                    ◇ A 10 7 5 3
                    ♣ K 7 6 2
```

At each table, North passed and East opened 1♠. South for Indonesia and Chinese Taipei passed. East-West reached 4♠ without interference and went one down. The New Zealand South bid 1NT ('comic'), a curious choice with that pattern, and also scored +50 against 4♠.

Would you rather be in 5◇ and take your chances on locating the ♡J for +400 or notch up a measly +50 against 4♠? China North-South had an admirable auction with South following Browne's **Rule of 15**:

WEST	NORTH	EAST	SOUTH
CC Chen	*Xiaojing*	*YH Chen*	*Weimin*
	No	1♠	Double
4♠	Double (1)	No	4NT (2)
Double (3)	5◇	All pass	

(1) Responsive, showing values, inviting a takeout with good shape
(2) Offering a choice of suits (not Blackwood)
(3) Showing values and suggesting penalties

In a perfect world, North would have the ♡J instead of the ◇J so that 5◇ would be laydown. Sad to relate, declarer mispicked the hearts and went one down. That was 3 Imps to Chinese Taipei, but China had the last laugh. They won the championship.

Use *S. & M.* to inflict pain

WEST	Dealer East : Both vulnerable
♠ 9 5 3	
♡ Q J 7 4	
◇ 6 4	
♣ Q 9 8 5	

WEST	NORTH	EAST	SOUTH
		1◇	2♣
No	No	Double	No
?			

What action would you take as West?

No one would criticise you for replying to partner's takeout double with 2♡, but if you are conscious of **S. & M.** you are more likely to find the winning action of passing for penalties. Occasionally you may come a cropper by leaving the double in, but most of the time you are on the way to a juicy penalty.

To pass a low-level takeout double and convert it to penalties, you need:

> **S**trong trumps **&** **M**isfit with partner's suit

It would be nice to have stronger clubs to leave the double in and a singleton in diamonds would be more attractive but their lack of bidding indicates partner is likely to be strong. The full deal:

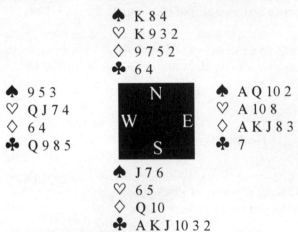

```
              ♠ K 8 4
              ♡ K 9 3 2
              ◇ 9 7 5 2
              ♣ 6 4
♠ 9 5 3        N          ♠ A Q 10 2
♡ Q J 7 4   W     E       ♡ A 10 8
◇ 6 4                     ◇ A K J 8 3
♣ Q 9 8 5      S          ♣ 7
              ♠ J 7 6
              ♡ 6 5
              ◇ Q 10
              ♣ A K J 10 3 2
```

Maybe East-West can reach 3NT, maybe not. Maybe 3NT makes, maybe not, but defending 2♣ doubled is a whole lot easier and loads more fun. Several lines lead to +800 for East-West. Try **S. & M.** Enjoy.

E.N.W.R.A.P.S.

What does partner's double mean in each of these auctions?

W	N	E	S	W	N	E	S
1♦	Dble	1♠	Dble . . .	1♠	No	1NT	No
				2♣	Dble . . .		

It is essential to be able to distinguish between a takeout double and a penalty double since their meanings are opposite. A takeout double says, 'Please bid' and a penalty double says, 'Please pass'. Over the last two decades, doubles that were once clearly for penalties have become takeout. Based on frequency and the need to be competitive, the standard for most top players is that all doubles at a low level are for takeout unless specified to be for penalties.

The question then arises, 'Which doubles are for penalties and how do I remember them?' **E.N.W.R.A.P.S.** covers the situations where doubles are played as penalties:

E.	To	**E**xpose a psyche
N.	After a	**N**o-trump bid
W.	After a	**W**eak-two or higher pre-empt by partner
R.	After a	**R**edouble
A.	After an	**A**rtificial bid
P.	After a	**P**revious penalty pass
S.		**S**ubsequent double after earlier pass of same suit

Expose a psyche

W	N	E	S	After a takeout double, a psyche in a
1♦	Dble	1♠	Dble . . .	major by third hand is common.

South's double is for penalties in spades and indicates that South was intending to bid spades. A later spade bid by South is natural. There is no great need for South to double for takeout here. South can simply bid 2♥ with hearts or 2♣ with clubs.

The principle: If partner has made a takeout double and third player changes suit, advancer's double is for penalties. This is not a responsive double situation. The responsive double, for takeout, occurs after partner has made a takeout double and third hand *raises opener's suit*.

Doubles of **N**o-trumps and after **N**o-trump bids

W	N	E	S	
1NT	Dble . . .			Most play that the double of a 1NT opening is for penalties.

W	N	E	S	
1NT	2♠	Dble . . .		Most play that the double of a suit bid is for penalties after a 1NT opening.

W	N	E	S	
1♠	2NT	Dble . . .		Most play that the double of a 2NT overcall (minors or other two-suiter) indicates a desire for penalties. All later doubles are for penalties.

After a **W**eak two or higher-pre-empt by partner

W	N	E	S	
2♥	3♦	Dble . . .		One of the aims of pre-empting is to lure the opponents into an indiscretion.

After a **R**edouble

W	N	E	S	
1♠	Dble	Rdble	2♣	The redouble indicates 10+ HCP and a misfit with opener's suit. All later doubles are for penalties.
No	No	Dble . . .		

The redouble itself suggests that penalties is the way to go. When South runs to 2♣, West should double with strong clubs, else pass and give partner the chance to double. A shortage in partner's suit and a strong 4+ holding in their suit are the penalty indicators (see **S** & **M**, page 40).

After an **A**rtificial bid

W	N	E	S	
1NT	No	2♣	Dble	South's double, showing strong clubs, is also known as 'lead-directing', but South is happy to defend 2♣ doubled.

W	N	E	S	
1♠	2♠	Dble . . .		North's 2♠ is a Michaels Cue-Bid, showing 5+ hearts and a 5+ minor.

Some play that East's double of 2♠ shows spades but it works better to use the double to indicate the desire for penalties. East's hand type will be similar to a redouble: 10+ HCP, misfit with partner and strong in at least one of their suits. All later doubles are for penalties.

After a **P**revious penalty pass

W	N	E	S	West's first double was for takeout. East's pass of the double was for penalties. Once a desire for penalties has been revealed, all later doubles are for penalties.
1◇	1♠	No	No	
Dble	No	No	2♣	
Dble . . .				

Subsequent double after previous pass of the same suit

W	N	E	S	East's double is for penalties. East had the chance to double 1♠ for takeout. After declining that opportunity, East's later double of spades is for penalties.
1◇	1♠	No	1NT	
No	2♠	Dble . . .		

W	N	E	S	Similarly, East had the chance to double 2♣ but passed. East's later double of clubs is for penalties.
1♠	2♣	No	No	
2♠	3♣	Dble . . .		

E.N.W.R.A.P.S. is not a matter of right or wrong. It simply provides an easy way to remember partnership agreements about penalty doubles. If your partnership has a different set of agreements, you can just create your own acronym to aid your memory. Suppose that you do not want to use a double to expose a psyche:

W	N	E	S	Perhaps you prefer South's double to indicate values but with no clear-cut bid, and so double is for takeout.
1◇	Dble	1♠	Dble . . .	

Simply remove **E** from **E.N.W.R.A.P.S.** and re-arrange the remaining letters to come up with **P.R.A.W.N.S.**. Indeed, if it makes it easier to remember, there is nothing wrong in changing **E.N.W.R.A.P.S.** into **P.P.R.A.W.N.S.**:

P.		**P**syche exposure
P.	After a	**P**revious penalty pass
R.	After a	**R**edouble
A.	After an	**A**rtificial bid
W.	After a	**W**eak-two or higher pre-empt by partner
N.	After a	**N**o-trump bid
S.		**S**ubsequent double after earlier pass of same suit

10 to 4 — <u>T</u>ime to <u>F</u>ly

1.	WEST ♠ J 6 5 4 2 ♡ J 10 9 5 4 ◇ J 9 ♣ 3	Dealer East : North-South vulnerable

WEST	NORTH	EAST	SOUTH
		1♠	No
?			
What action would you take as West?			

2.	WEST ♠ Q 8 7 3 ♡ 6 3 ◇ K 8 7 4 2 ♣ 5 2	Dealer East : Both vulnerable

WEST	NORTH	EAST	SOUTH
		2♠*	No
?			
*weak two What should West do here?			

If you wish to be a thorn in the enemy's side, you must take maximum pre-emptive action when your side has a strong trump fit. Your aim is to prevent the opponents from finding their best spot.

10 to 4 means that *if you know that your side has, or is likely to have, ten trumps, bid to the four-level at once.* With **10** trumps, bid **4**.

On both the above problems, West should jump to 4♠ at once. #1 will re-appear in **ATP DAFT** (see page 55). The full deal for #2 reveals that N-S can make 6♡ or 5♣ while declarer can hold 4♠ doubled to –200. Bid 4♠ and let them try to sort it out if they can.

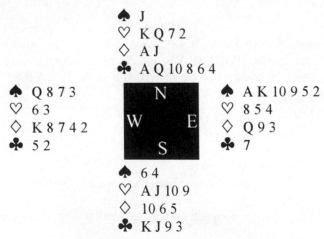

S.I.T.E.S. T.O.X.I.C.

Each of the following problems arose in a national or international teams championship. The answers would not be different if the setting were a pairs event.

1. EAST	Dealer North : Nil vulnerable			
♠ 7	WEST	NORTH	EAST	SOUTH
♡ A K 6 4 2		No	1♡	1♠
◇ Q 4	No	No	?	
♣ K J 9 8 4	What action would you take as East?			

2. What would you do as East with these cards:	Dealer South : Nil vulnerable			
	WEST	NORTH	EAST	SOUTH
				2◇ (1)
♠ 6	No	2♡ (2)	No	2♠ (3)
♡ Q 10 6 4	No	No	?	
◇ A K J 4	(1) Multi-2◇			
♣ Q 7 6 5	(2) 'Pass if you have a weak two in hearts.'			
	(3) 'I have a weak two in spades.'			

3. What action would you take as East?	Dealer South : Both vulnerable			
	WEST	NORTH	EAST	SOUTH
♠ K 10 4 2				1NT (1)
♡ 9	No	2◇ (2)	No	2♡
◇ K J 7 6	No	No	?	
♣ 10 8 5 2	(1) 15-17 (2) Transfer to hearts			

4. WEST	Dealer South : Both vulnerable			
♠ K J 6	WEST	NORTH	EAST	SOUTH
♡ Q 9 8 7 5				1NT (1)
◇ A 2	Dble (2)	2♣ (3)	No	2◇
♣ A K 8	?			
What should West do at this point?	(1) 12-14 (2) For penalties			
	(3) Clubs and another suit			

45

S.	**S**hort	If you derive no other benefit from this book, you will still be well ahead if you regularly employ **S.I.T.E.S. T.O.X.I.C.** to assist you in your competitive decisions. When you wish to compete, the most flexible action is the takeout double and, almost always, a takeout double will give the best result if you have a shortage in the enemy suit. The shortage itself should ring a bell that double is the way to go. *Shortage means Double.*
I.	**I**n	
T.	**T**he	
E.	**E**nemy	
S.	**S**uit?	
T.	**T**ake	
O.	**O**ut	
X.	**X** = Double	
I.	**I**s	
C.	**C**orrect.	

1. This arose during a qualifying round of the 1998 Australian Grand National Open Teams:

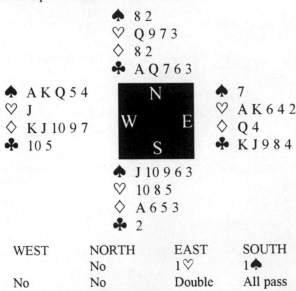

```
                    ♠ 8 2
                    ♡ Q 9 7 3
                    ◇ 8 2
                    ♣ A Q 7 6 3
  ♠ A K Q 5 4                       ♠ 7
  ♡ J              N                ♡ A K 6 4 2
  ◇ K J 10 9 7   W     E            ◇ Q 4
  ♣ 10 5            S               ♣ K J 9 8 4
                    ♠ J 10 9 6 3
                    ♡ 10 8 5
                    ◇ A 6 5 3
                    ♣ 2
```

WEST	NORTH	EAST	SOUTH
	No	1♡	1♠
No	No	Double	All pass

South scored two trump tricks and two aces for three down. −500 was a salutary lesson not to overcall on tram tickets. (Had North run from 1♠ doubled to 2♣, East would double for penalties — see the **P** in **ENWRAPS** at page 43.) At the other table, a more disciplined South passed and 3NT by East was reached. South led the ♠J, taken in dummy, and ducked when a diamond was led to the queen. On winning the next diamond, South shifted to a heart and dummy was dead. Two down.

2. This problem occurred in the 1996 Open Teams Olympiad in the Indonesia v New Zealand match from the qualifying rounds.

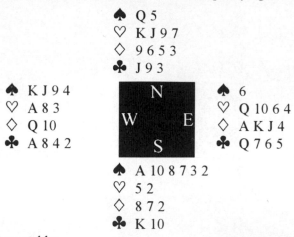

```
                    ♠ Q 5
                    ♡ K J 9 7
                    ◇ 9 6 5 3
                    ♣ J 9 3
  ♠ K J 9 4                        ♠ 6
  ♡ A 8 3           N              ♡ Q 10 6 4
  ◇ Q 10        W       E          ◇ A K J 4
  ♣ A 8 4 2          S             ♣ Q 7 6 5
                    ♠ A 10 8 7 3 2
                    ♡ 5 2
                    ◇ 8 7 2
                    ♣ K 10
```

At one table:

WEST	NORTH	EAST	SOUTH
Sacul	*Blackstock*	*Karwur*	*Yule*
			2♠
No	No	Double	All pass

Declining to lead from an ace-high suit in a trump contract, Sacul started with the ◇Q and shortly thereafter declarer was three off, −500. This did not figure to be expensive as 3NT is on for East-West. However:

WEST	NORTH	EAST	SOUTH
			2◇
No	2♡	No	2♠
No	No	No??	

2◇ was a multi, 2♡ was 'Pass or Correct' and 2♠ confirmed a weak two opening in spades. Declarer here went two down, −100, +9 Imps to Indonesia who went on to reach the final (losing to France) while New Zealand narrowly missed the quarter-finals (by one Victory Point).

After a multi, treat a weak response or a weak rebid by the opener as though it were the opening bid. One suspects that East was away with the pixies. Had he focussed on **SITES TOXIC**, the double would have been automatic.

3. This came up in the final of the 1998 Vanderbilt (USA National Open Teams Championship):

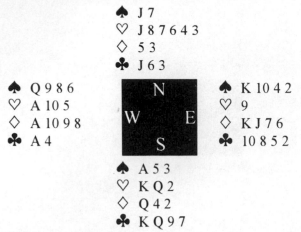

```
              ♠ J 7
              ♡ J 8 7 6 4 3
              ◇ 5 3
              ♣ J 6 3
♠ Q 9 8 6          N          ♠ K 10 4 2
♡ A 10 5                      ♡ 9
◇ A 10 9 8    W       E       ◇ K J 7 6
♣ A 4              S          ♣ 10 8 5 2
              ♠ A 5 3
              ♡ K Q 2
              ◇ Q 4 2
              ♣ K Q 9 7
```

At both tables:

WEST	NORTH	EAST	SOUTH
Stansby	*Passell*	*Martel*	*Seamon*
Burger	*Goldman*	*Cayne*	*Soloway*
			1NT
No	2◇	No	2♡
No	No	No	

2♡ cannot be defeated and Goldman-Soloway notched up +1 Imp for an overtrick. The difference between East's failure to take action here and the New Zealand inaction on Problem #2 is only a matter of degree.

SITES TOXIC points the way. If East doubles, for takeout of course, West will bid 2♠ where ten tricks can be made. North-South might push on to 3♡, which can be defeated via a spade lead or by leading the ♣A and scoring a club ruff later. It is too much to expect to reach 4♠ but passing out 2♡ is timid indeed. It cost 5-7 Imps here and it does not take many such swings to decide a match.

How do you account for the meekness of such powerful East players? Perhaps the fear of reprisals for incurring –500 or –800 may play a part. Passing will lead to a small minus, which will leave you with a clear conscience at score-up time. Thus, 'conscience doth make cowards of us all'.

4. This too arose in the final of the 1998 Vanderbilt:

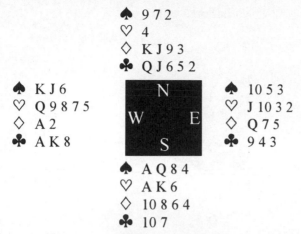

```
              ♠ 9 7 2
              ♡ 4
              ◇ K J 9 3
              ♣ Q J 6 5 2
♠ K J 6            N            ♠ 10 5 3
♡ Q 9 8 7 5                     ♡ J 10 3 2
◇ A 2          W       E        ◇ Q 7 5
♣ A K 8            S            ♣ 9 4 3
              ♠ A Q 8 4
              ♡ A K 6
              ◇ 10 8 6 4
              ♣ 10 7
```

At one table:

WEST	NORTH	EAST	SOUTH
			1◇
1♡	2◇	No	No
Dble	3♣	3♡	All pass

North led a diamond and dummy's queen won. A heart from dummy saw South win and shift to a low spade, run to dummy's 10. Declarer had no further problems. A shift to the ♣10 looks more appealing, especially on the bidding. West wins and leads a heart but if South ducks this, declarer lacks the entries to play spades twice from dummy. To make 3♡, declarer needs to lead a spade from dummy at trick 2.

At the other table:

WEST	NORTH	EAST	SOUTH
			1NT - - - 12-14
Dble	2♣	No	2◇ All pass

East-West missed their 9-card heart fit and allowed North-South to play in 2◇ which just made. **SITES TOXIC** will help. West, *short in the enemy suit*, should double for takeout. East will bid 2♡ and North-South cannot win the board. Playing the double for takeout here is sensible but you need to amend the **N** in **ENWRAPS** (pages 41 – 43) so that the double of no-trumps is penalties but the double of a suit runout is for takeout.

Once you accept **SITES TOXIC**, deals like this present no problems:

Dealer East : North-South vulnerable

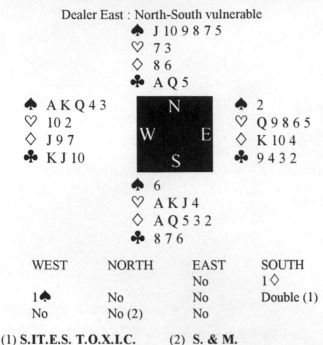

```
                    ♠ J 10 9 8 7 5
                    ♡ 7 3
                    ◇ 8 6
                    ♣ A Q 5
  ♠ A K Q 4 3              ♠ 2
  ♡ 10 2                   ♡ Q 9 8 6 5
  ◇ J 9 7                  ◇ K 10 4
  ♣ K J 10                 ♣ 9 4 3 2
                    ♠ 6
                    ♡ A K J 4
                    ◇ A Q 5 3 2
                    ♣ 8 7 6
```

WEST	NORTH	EAST	SOUTH
		No	1◇
1♠	No	No	Double (1)
No	No (2)	No	

(1) **S.IT.E.S. T.O.X.I.C.**   (2) **S. & M.**

North leads the ◇8. South takes two diamond tricks and gives North a diamond ruff with the ◇5 (suit-preference for hearts). Alternatively, after winning the first diamond, South can cash the king of hearts to show the outside entry.

After ruffing the diamond, North might well simply lead spades from the top (and might indeed have led a top spade initially). After coming in with a heart, a club switch will give the defence all their tricks. West will be doing well to make more than four tricks.

South does not double in the knowledge that North will pass for penalties (although that is a common outcome in such auctions if opener is minimum) but simply to find the best spot for the partnership. With a nondescript hand, partner will answer the double. If hearts is the right contract, double will locate it. If diamonds is best, North can bid diamonds in reply to the double. Even clubs might be best. Partner's pass for penalties is a bonus.

Similarly:

Dealer North : Nil vulnerable

```
                  ♠ Q 10 9 4
                  ♡ J 6 5 4 2
                  ◇ Q J 7
                  ♣ J
♠ 3                              ♠ A J 7 6 2
♡ 9 8 3                          ♡ A K 10
◇ A 10 5 3 2                     ◇ 8 6 4
♣ A 6 4 2                        ♣ 8 3
                  ♠ K 8 5
                  ♡ Q 7
                  ◇ K 9
                  ♣ K Q 10 9 7 5
```

WEST	NORTH	EAST	SOUTH
	No	1♠	2♣
No	No	Double (1)	All pass

(1) S.IT.E.S. T.O.X.I.C.

In days of yore, East, with nothing extra, would pass out 2♣. Nowadays one passes only if strong in the overcalled suit.

West's trumps are nothing special but the singleton in partner's suit makes it attractive to try a speculative pass for penalties. Having the ♣A, West will have another chance to locate East's entry even if East does not have the ♠A. West scores two ruffs to take 2♣ doubled two down. +300 is a definite improvement on the score available for E-W in diamonds.

What about this auction:

WEST	Dealer West : Nil vulnerable			
♠ A 10 8 4 2	WEST	NORTH	EAST	SOUTH
♡ A K Q 4	1♠	No	1NT	2◇
◇ 5	?			
♣ 5 4 3	What should West do now?			

51

Dealer West : Nil vulnerable

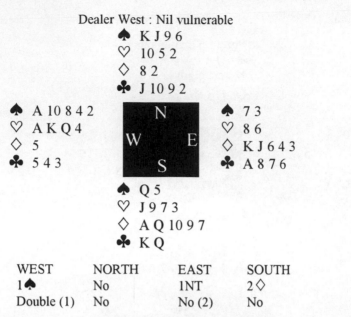

```
                  ♠ K J 9 6
                  ♡ 10 5 2
                  ◇ 8 2
                  ♣ J 10 9 2
  ♠ A 10 8 4 2          ♠ 7 3
  ♡ A K Q 4             ♡ 8 6
  ◇ 5                   ◇ K J 6 4 3
  ♣ 5 4 3               ♣ A 8 7 6
                  ♠ Q 5
                  ♡ J 9 7 3
                  ◇ A Q 10 9 7
                  ♣ K Q
```

WEST	NORTH	EAST	SOUTH
1♠	No	1NT	2◇
Double (1)	No	No (2)	No

(1) <u>S</u>hort <u>I</u>n <u>T</u>he <u>E</u>nemy <u>S</u>uit, <u>T</u>ake <u>O</u>ut <u>X</u> <u>I</u>s <u>C</u>orrect   (2) **S. & M.**

A West player not imbued with the **SITES TOXIC** spirit might compete with 2♡ over 2◇. East would give preference to 2♠ and unless some miracle occurs, West will lose one diamond, two clubs and three trump tricks for one down. Such a West fails to realise that if 2♡ is the right spot for East-West, double will find the 2♡ contract.

Furthermore, rebidding 2♡ focuses only on the major suits. For all West knows, the best spot for East-West might be in clubs. Double will allow you to find that while 2♡ will not. Finally, if East happens to be strong in diamonds, you can play for penalties.

Against 2◇ doubled, West starts with four rounds of hearts. East discards a spade on the third round and over-ruffs dummy's ◇8 on the fourth round. A spade to the ace and a spade ruff is followed by the ♣A. East still has a trump trick to come and that means three down, +500.

Now, tell me honestly, would you rather struggle vainly in 2♠ or take the opponents to the cleaners? Remember, **SITES TOXIC** spells poison to the opponents.

A.T.P. D.A.F.T.

Are The Politicians Doing Anything For Taxpayers

1.	WEST	Dealer South : Both vulnerable

		WEST	NORTH	EAST	SOUTH
	♠ - - -				4♠
	♡ Q 10 7	?			
	◇ A K 6 2				
	♣ A K Q 9 7 5	What action would you take as West?			

2.	SOUTH	Dealer West : North-South vulnerable

		WEST	NORTH	EAST	SOUTH
	♠ - - -	1♠	No	4♠	?
	♡ A K 2	What would you do as South?			
	◇ A 10 8 4				
	♣ A K J 7 5 4				

3.	WEST	Dealer North : Nil vulnerable

		WEST	NORTH	EAST	SOUTH
	♠ A K J 10 2		1◇	No	1♡
	♡ - - -	Dble	4♡	No	No
	◇ Q 10 7	?			
	♣ K Q J 9 4	What would you do now as West?			

4.	EAST	Dealer East : Nil vulnerable

		WEST	NORTH	EAST	SOUTH
	♠ A 10 6 3			1♣	4♡
	♡ 2	No	No	?	
	◇ 6 3	What would you do as East?			
	♣ A Q 9 6 4 2				

5.	WEST	Dealer North : East-West vulnerable

		WEST	NORTH	EAST	SOUTH
	♠ - - -		No	1NT (1)	4♠
	♡ A 9 8 7 2	?			
	◇ K Q 10 2				
	♣ J 10 9 3	What would you do as West? (1) 15-17			

Once you recognise the value of **SITES TOXIC**, you will want to extend it to higher levels. The most effective weapon against pre-empts is to double for takeout. You may miss an occasional penalty but you cater effectively for the more common situations where you are short in the pre-emptor's suit. The inhibiting factor may be your upbringing when you learnt that doubles at the high levels are for penalties. Throw off those shackles and you will win more often. Don't be daft : play **ATP DAFT**:

A.	After	Are
T.	They	The
P.	Pre-empt,	Politicians
D.	Doubles	Doing
A.	Are	Anything
F.	For	For
T.	Takeout	Taxpayers

ATP DAFT applies whether it is a pre-emptive opening, overcall or raise. How high should doubles of pre-empts be for takeout? As high as you dare . . . and then some more. At the very least, play them up to the 5◇ level, and higher than that if you can find a willing partner.

1. In a major teams event, several Wests opted for 5♣. Not a success:

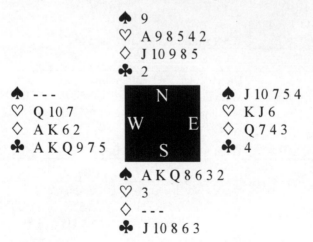

♠ 9
♡ A 9 8 5 4 2
◇ J 10 9 8 5
♣ 2

♠ - - -
♡ Q 10 7
◇ A K 6 2
♣ A K Q 9 7 5

♠ J 10 7 5 4
♡ K J 6
◇ Q 7 4 3
♣ 4

♠ A K Q 8 6 3 2
♡ 3
◇ - - -
♣ J 10 8 6 3

The 5♣ bidders all failed while those who doubled found East delighted to pass. 5♣ puts all your eggs in one basket. Doubles increases the options.

2. Bid 5♣ and you play it there, but you are still a long way from par.

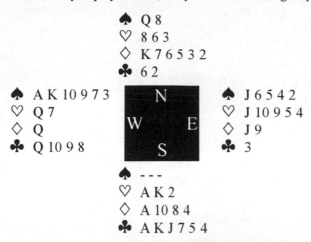

     ♠ Q 8
     ♡ 8 6 3
     ◇ K 7 6 5 3 2
     ♣ 6 2

♠ A K 10 9 7 3   ♠ J 6 5 4 2
♡ Q 7   ♡ J 10 9 5 4
◇ Q   ◇ J 9
♣ Q 10 9 8   ♣ 3

     ♠ - - -
     ♡ A K 2
     ◇ A 10 8 4
     ♣ A K J 7 5 4

This is the aftermath of **10 to 4 #1** (page 44). After 1♠ : No : 4♠, Double by South is best as long as it is for takeout. North should bid 5◇ and South has a comfortable 6◇ raise. That was worth +11 Imps as the datum was North-South +820. Note that 4♠ doubled is only –100, a real bonanza against the possible vulnerable grand slam in diamonds.

3.

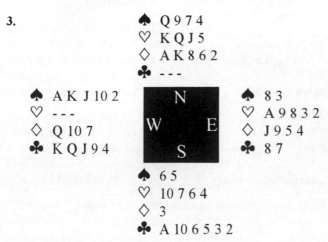

     ♠ Q 9 7 4
     ♡ K Q J 5
     ◇ A K 8 6 2
     ♣ - - -

♠ A K J 10 2   ♠ 8 3
♡ - - -   ♡ A 9 8 3 2
◇ Q 10 7   ◇ J 9 5 4
♣ K Q J 9 4   ♣ 8 7

     ♠ 6 5
     ♡ 10 7 6 4
     ◇ 3
     ♣ A 10 6 5 3 2

If you bid 4♠, North doubles and you are –500. If you double again for takeout, the outcome is a happier one (although it may not always be so).

4.   Dealer East : Nil vulnerable
                          ♠ K J 2
                          ♡ 6
                          ◇ Q J 10 8 5 4
                          ♣ J 10 5

♠ Q 9 8 5 4   ♠ A 10 6 3
♡ K 5 4 3   ♡ 2
◇ 9 7 2      ◇ 6 3
♣ 8   ♣ A Q 9 6 4 2

                          ♠ 7
                          ♡ A Q J 10 9 8 7
                          ◇ A K
                          ♣ K 7 3

The deal comes from the semi-finals of the 1996 Open Teams Olympiad. This was the auction at one of the tables in Denmark v Indonesia:

WEST	NORTH	EAST	SOUTH
		1♣	4♡
No	No	Double	No
4♠	No	No	Double
No	No	No	

Notice that East was doing all the right things: *With 6-4, bid more* and **SITES TOXIC** and **A**fter **T**hey **P**re-empt, **D**oubles **A**re **F**or **T**akeout. South was unusually strong even for a pre-empt after an opening bid but East-West would have come out on top if West had just followed **S. & M.**

West had a **M**isfit with partner and **S**trength in the opponent's suit. West should have left the double in and led a club. East takes the ♣A and returns the ♣9 (suit-preference signal), ruffed. A spade to the ace, a second club ruff plus the ♡K later will give East-West five tricks and +300. That is a pretty handy result when East-West have only 15 HCP.

If East were significantly stronger (so that 4♠ might make), the penalty would have been greater. As it was, the Danish West went two down for –300 instead of being +300. Indonesia won the semi-final 230-226. There is a lesson here: If partner makes a takeout double and you have an **S. & M.** hand, take the money. Pass for penalties.

5.   Dealer North : East-West vulnerable

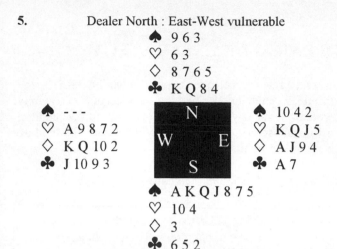

                    ♠ 9 6 3
                    ♡ 6 3
                    ◇ 8 7 6 5
                    ♣ K Q 8 4

♠ - - -   ♠ 10 4 2
♡ A 9 8 7 2   ♡ K Q J 5
◇ K Q 10 2   ◇ A J 9 4
♣ J 10 9 3   ♣ A 7

                    ♠ A K Q J 8 7 5
                    ♡ 10 4
                    ◇ 3
                    ♣ 6 5 2

This deal arose in the 1998 Pacific Asian Teams Championships. Using **ATP DAFT**, the auction might reasonably go:

WEST	NORTH	EAST	SOUTH
	No	1NT	4♠
Double (1)	No	4NT (2)	No
5♠	No	6◇	All pass

(1) **A**fter **T**hey **P**re-empt, **D**oubles **A**re **F**or **T**akeout
(2) Playable in two suits (and not much in spades, else the double would be left in).
(3) 'Pick a slam. I have the spades under control.'

6♡ or 6◇ is a good slam. Thirteen tricks can be made in diamonds on a spade lead but not on a top club lead (because the diamonds are 4-1). 7◇ is not a great slam. Be satisfied to reach the good small slam.

In the women's match between Australia v New Zealand, the bidding with Australia East-West went (No) : 1◇ : (4♠) : 5◇, all pass. At the other table, the NZ East opened 1NT and South jumped to 4♠. This exploited a weakness in the NZ methods as their takeout doubles stopped at 4♡. West's double was systemically for penalties and so East naturally passed. Declarer always has eight tricks in 4♠ and so the penalty was only –300. Is the message coming through? *Play takeout doubles as high as you dare . . . and then some more!*

CHAPTER 6

OPENING LEAD STRATEGY

The first port of call when considering your opening lead is the bidding. You should be studying the bidding as it occurs, not merely after the auction is over, for if you fail to pay attention to the bidding, you have lost a valuable source of information. Sometimes the bidding itself points the way to the right suit to lead.

S.P.A.T.S. provides a good drill after you have studied the bidding.

S.	Sequence to lead? Probably best.
P.	Passive lead? Often indicated by the bidding.
A.	Attacking lead? Again often revealed in the bidding.
T.	Trump lead? See **F.U.N.D.S.** and **T.T.T.T.T.T.T.T.T.**
S.	Singleton lead? **W.H.A.T.** is a good guide.

Sequence To Lead?

A sequence is so attractive because it has the potential to establish winners without giving declarer undeserved tricks. The longer the sequence, the greater the safety. 10-9-8-7 is safer than Q-J-6. The stronger the sequence, the better the prospects. K-Q-J-x is obviously a more potent source of tricks than J-10-9-x. In a trump contract, a suit headed by A-K is a powerful start since you (presumably) win the trick without yet having set up a trick for declarer. Being able to see dummy and partner's signal on your lead provide valuable clues how to continue.

Passive Lead?

A passive lead is from a suit with no honour card, either from three or more rags or from two or three worthless trumps. The aim of a passive lead is not to set up tricks but hopefully to avoid giving away a trick. Leading from a suit headed by one honour or two broken honours (such as from K-J-x-x) is risky; leading from a worthless suit is safer.

With no clear-cut, strong lead, a passive lead is indicated when a 1NT or 2NT opening is passed out, after an invitational auction or when there is no evidence of a long suit in dummy. **Death With Honour** deals with another area where a passive lead is usually best:

Death With Honour

I am surprised how often average players choose to lead against 6NT as though they were leading against 3NT. To defeat a game or a part-score, you need to set up several tricks. Against a grand slam, you need only one trick. Against 6NT, two tricks will do. It is very risky to lead away from an unsupported honour against a grand slam or against 6NT. As declarer and dummy have so much strength, a lead from a king-high or queen-high suit figures to hand declarer an extra trick.

You will rarely be lucky enough to have a sequence to lead at this level. If you do, your worries are over. If not, prefer a worthless suit of three or more cards, even if that suit has been bid by the opponents.

A trump lead from three or more rags is unlikely to cost against a grand slam. Against 6NT, to lead from x-x-x or longer in a suit which they have bid and raised is also virtually risk-free.

To lead from a suit with one or two honours against 6NT can be fatal. A suit with no honours is much safer. *Prefer to live with honour.*

MUD, LOT, TON and TONAR

These refer to methods of leading from rag cards. **MUD** stands for **M**iddle – **U**p – **D**own, meaning that you lead the middle card first and play the high card next. For example, from 8-7-3, start with the 7 and play the 8 on the next round. From 5-4-2, lead the 4 and play the 5 next. The aim is to distinguish three cards from doubleton leads (where you lead highest, then lower on the next round, such as 7-then-3). Low-then-higher (7-then-8, for example) shows more than two cards.

MUD is the most popular method among average players but has the drawback of ambiguity until the second round is played. The **MUD** card could be a singleton, from a doubleton or from 3+ cards. If partner needs to know your length from the first lead, **MUD** cannot provide the answer.

LOT (**L**owest **O**f **T**hree) is popular among experts. If the card can be seen to be lowest, it can be a singleton or from three but not a doubleton. **LOT** can deny a doubleton with the first card, while **MUD** cannot do this. The drawback of **LOT** is that lowest can be from three rags or from three to an honour and partner cannot tell which. When playing **MUD**, leading the lowest card is either a singleton or promises an honour card.

The aim of **TON** (<u>T</u>op <u>O</u>f <u>N</u>othing) is to deny an honour card in the suit led but it is the most despised style of leads because partner cannot tell whether the lead is from a doubleton, from three cards or from more than three. You should shy away from **TON** in a suit contract since it can be vital for partner to know that you hold a doubleton and can ruff the third round. **TON** can be useful against no-trumps because it is inappropriate to lead from a singleton or a doubleton in an unbid suit.

Since the lead in no-trumps is from length, **TON** informs partner that your suit is long but has no honour card strength. That may direct partner to switch to a more fruitful source of tricks instead of relentlessly pursuing your worthless suit. As one player put it: 'The trouble with my partner is that he keeps returning my rotten leads.'

There can even be a place for <u>T</u>op <u>O</u>f <u>N</u>othing in a suit contract:

TONAR stands for <u>T</u>op <u>O</u>f <u>N</u>othing <u>A</u>fter <u>R</u>aise. Since the main criticism levelled against **TON** is that it fails to distinguish doubletons from longer holdings, it makes sense to use **TON** when you cannot hold a doubleton. If you have raised partner's suit and thus shown 4- or 3-card support, by all means lead <u>T</u>op <u>O</u>f <u>N</u>othing. **TONAR** is a sensible method.

Attacking Lead?

An attacking lead is from a suit which has one or two honours but less than a 3+ sequence. An attacking lead is risky as it may present declarer with an undeserved trick.

A 10 3 *(dummy)*

J 7 6 2   Q 8 5

K 9 4

Declarer has two tricks but if either defender broaches this suit, declarer can score three.

Nevertheless, if the need arises, you must be prepared to take the risk. The bidding holds the clues. Quite often, there is only one unbid suit. If that suit is clearly the best start, lead it even if it is an attacking lead. It usually pays to make an attacking lead against a small slam in a suit, against strong opposition bidding, after a pre-empt or when dummy is known to hold a long suit. Two strong guides for attacking leads are **SSSAP** and **DILLUS**.

S.S.S.A.P.
Softly, Softly, Saints At Prayer

WEST	NORTH	EAST	SOUTH
	3♣	No	3NT
No	No	No	

What should West lead from:

    ♠ J 7 5 4   ♡ Q 8 5 3 2   ◇ A K 5   ♣ 7

Had they bid 1NT : 3NT, a heart lead would be normal. After a pre-empt, declarer usually succeeds by running the long suit. If the defenders do not score their tricks quickly, they do not come at all. There is not enough time to set up a long suit if you have to knock out two stoppers and then regain the lead to cash your tricks. Enter **SSSAP**:

S.	Strong	Softly,
S.	Short	Softly,
S.	Suit	Saints
A.	After	At
P.	Pre-empt	Prayer

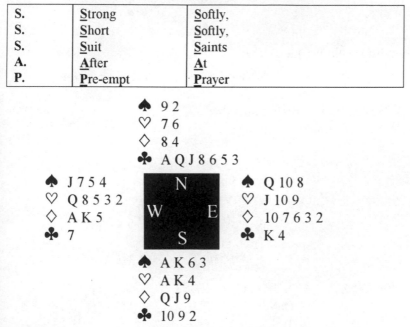

```
                    ♠ 9 2
                    ♡ 7 6
                    ◇ 8 4
                    ♣ A Q J 8 6 5 3
  ♠ J 7 5 4                          ♠ Q 10 8
  ♡ Q 8 5 3 2          N            ♡ J 10 9
  ◇ A K 5         W         E       ◇ 10 7 6 3 2
  ♣ 7                  S            ♣ K 4
                    ♠ A K 6 3
                    ♡ A K 4
                    ◇ Q J 9
                    ♣ 10 9 2
```

Using **SSSAP**, you find the diamond lead and beat 3NT. On any other lead, South has ten tricks. **SSSAP** is also valuable against suit contracts.

D.I.L.L. U.S.?
Do I Look Like Utterly Stupid?

1. Dealer North : Both vulnerable

WEST	NORTH	EAST	SOUTH
	1♣	No	1♡
No	2♣	No	3♡
No	4♡	All pass	

What should West lead from:

    ♠ J 7 3   ♡ 8 7 5   ◇ K J 7 2   ♣ 9 6 2

2. Dealer East : Both vulnerable

WEST	NORTH	EAST	SOUTH
		No	1♠
No	2♡	No	2♠
No	4♠	All pass	

What should West lead from:

    ♠ 10 7 3   ♡ 8 7 5 3   ◇ K 7 2   ♣ A 9 4

3. Dealer North : Both vulnerable

        ♠ Q 6 5
        ♡ 9 3
        ◇ A Q 10 7 4
        ♣ 6 5 4

                     ♠ A 9 8 3
                     ♡ 7 5 4
                     ◇ 6 5 2
                     ♣ J 3 2

WEST	NORTH	EAST	SOUTH	
	Pass	No	1♡	
1♠	1NT	No	4♡	All pass

West leads the J of spades, 5 from dummy. How should East defend?

4. Dealer South : Both vulnerable

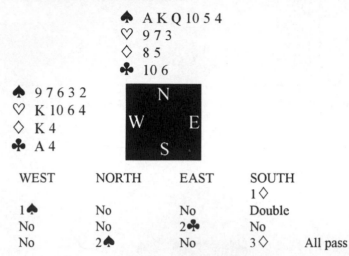

♠ A K Q 10 5 4
♡ 9 7 3
◇ 8 5
♣ 10 6

♠ 9 7 6 3 2
♡ K 10 6 4
◇ K 4
♣ A 4

WEST	NORTH	EAST	SOUTH	
			1 ◇	
1 ♠	No	No	Double	
No	No	2 ♣	No	
No	2 ♠	No	3 ◇	All pass

Are you as appalled as I am by that 1♠ overcall? The bidding is as it took place in the final of the 1998 Pacific Asian Women's Teams. West might profit from Tip 26 in *100 Winning Bridge Tips* on the Suit Quality Test for overcalls. North was no doubt salivating at the prospect of defending against 1♠ doubled but East ran to 2♣ and the contract became 3 ◇.

West leads the ace of clubs followed by a club to East's king. On the ♣3 at trick 3, South plays the queen and West ruffs with the king of diamonds, as dummy discards a heart. How should West continue?

****

When declarer has a useful long suit in dummy, what plan does declarer follow? The normal strategy is to draw trumps and then run the long suit to discard losers. When you are on lead against a trump contract where dummy has shown a long suit, you must not lead a trump since that plays right into declarer's plan. Likewise, leading dummy's long suit figures to help declarer rather than the defence.

If declarer has losers in trumps or in dummy's long suit, these will fall in your lap. The danger is that declarer's losers in the *outside* suits will vanish. When a strong, long suit is certain or likely to turn up in dummy, it is usually a sound move to lead an unbid suit. You must collect what tricks you can in these suits before declarer starts on the discarding. That is the basis of **D.I.L.L.U.S.**

D.	**D**ummy	**D**o
I.	**I**s	**I**
L.	**L**ong,	**L**ook
L.	**L**ead	**L**ike
U.	**U**nbid	**U**tterly
S.	**S**uit	**S**tupid?

Follow the **DILLUS** approach and you will look smart, not stupid.

You may now care to review your answers to questions 1-4 before looking at the complete deals.

1.

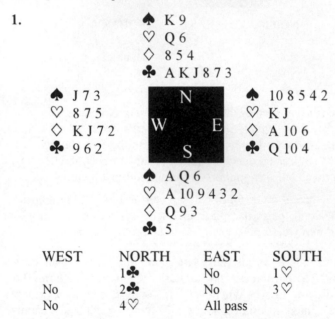

```
              ♠ K 9
              ♡ Q 6
              ◇ 8 5 4
              ♣ A K J 8 7 3
  ♠ J 7 3                    ♠ 10 8 5 4 2
  ♡ 8 7 5         N          ♡ K J
  ◇ K J 7 2    W     E       ◇ A 10 6
  ♣ 9 6 2         S          ♣ Q 10 4
              ♠ A Q 6
              ♡ A 10 9 4 3 2
              ◇ Q 9 3
              ♣ 5
```

WEST	NORTH	EAST	SOUTH
	1♣	No	1♡
No	2♣	No	3♡
No	4♡	All pass	

As dummy will turn up with five clubs, more commonly six, and West is weak in clubs, **D**ummy-**I**s-**L**ong, **L**ead-**U**nbid-**S**uit indicates the need to lead a spade or a diamond. A suit with two honours stands a much better chance of success than a suit with only one. West should lead the 2 of diamonds, and very swiftly the defence has three tricks with a trump trick to come.

A spade lead could work but it requires much more from partner than a diamond lead. On a non-diamond lead, declarer succeeds.

2.

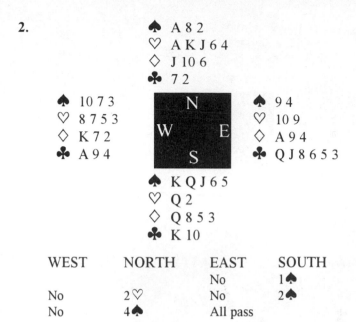

♠ A 8 2
♥ A K J 6 4
♦ J 10 6
♣ 7 2

♠ 10 7 3
♥ 8 7 5 3
♦ K 7 2
♣ A 9 4

♠ 9 4
♥ 10 9
♦ A 9 4
♣ Q J 8 6 5 3

♠ K Q J 6 5
♥ Q 2
♦ Q 8 5 3
♣ K 10

WEST	NORTH	EAST	SOUTH
		No	1♠
No	2♥	No	2♠
No	4♠	All pass	

The 2♥ response to 1♠ indicates a five-card or longer suit. With no useful cards in hearts, West should realise the danger of declarer pitching losers on the hearts. **DILLUS** applies and so West should lead one of the minors. Which one?

When choosing an unbid suit in a trump contact, one of which is headed by the ace (without the king as well) and the other has no ace, prefer the suit without the ace. Leading an ace tends to work out only if partner has the king, one useful card. Leading from a king has twice the success rate since there are two useful cards partner might hold, the ace or the queen. Here the lead should be the 2 of diamonds. To lead from a king is risky but **DILLUS** requires that such risks be taken.

After winning with the ace of diamonds, East needs to cooperate. West would lead the king from a K-Q combination and so East knows that West might hold the ♦K or the ♦Q but not both. As a diamond return can score only one more trick at best, East should shift to clubs, leading the queen. That is the best hope of defeating the contract.

Note that declarer has ten tricks on the ♣A lead and diamond switch. On a 'safe' (?) major suit lead, declarer has eleven tricks.

3.

WEST	NORTH	EAST	SOUTH
	Pass	No	1♡
1♠	1NT	No	4♡	All pass

Sometimes the long suit in dummy is not revealed in the bidding but becomes obvious when dummy appears. That is the situation here.

East is not worth a 2♠ raise and is happy to defend against 1NT (which can be defeated by two tricks after a low spade lead). West did well to avoid a trump lead ('do not lead a trump if dummy has not promised support' — see **F.U.N.D.S.**, page 68) and to start with the jack of spades when no suit offered an attractive lead.

East needs to be **DILLUS**-conscious. With the diamonds threatening to provide discards (if declarer lacks the king, any finesse in diamonds is working), there is considerable urgency in collecting the tricks for the defence. As West figures to have five spades, South will have only a singleton and the defence can come to only one spade trick. Only the clubs offer any hope of extra tricks.

East should rise with the ace of spades, even though the jack is highly likely to win the trick, and switch to the *jack* of clubs. Since you need three club tricks, you must pray West has A-Q-10 and then leading the jack becomes essential. If East shifts to a low club, declarer can play low from hand and the defence now makes only one spade and two clubs.

4.

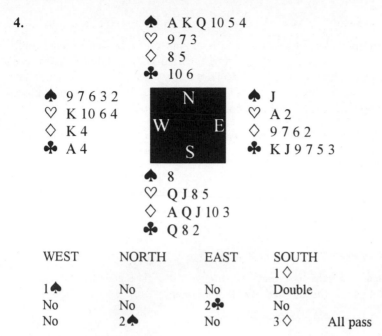

```
                    ♠ A K Q 10 5 4
                    ♡ 9 7 3
                    ◇ 8 5
                    ♣ 10 6
  ♠ 9 7 6 3 2              N              ♠ J
  ♡ K 10 6 4                               ♡ A 2
  ◇ K 4           W              E         ◇ 9 7 6 2
  ♣ A 4                    S              ♣ K J 9 7 5 3
                    ♠ 8
                    ♡ Q J 8 5
                    ◇ A Q J 10 3
                    ♣ Q 8 2
```

WEST	NORTH	EAST	SOUTH
			1 ◇
1 ♠	No	No	Double
No	No	2 ♣	No
No	2 ♠	No	3 ◇	All pass

After East's rescue to 2♣, West led the ace of clubs followed by a club to the king. The third round of clubs was ruffed by the king of diamonds as dummy discarded a heart. West exited with a trump and as declarer drew trumps, West discarded spades, hoping that South had a spade void. After four rounds of trumps declarer played spades from the top and made ten tricks.

If East were void in spades, the ♣J would have been led at trick 3 as a suit preference for spades. A low club indicates interest in the lower suit outside trumps, a heart. With a singleton spade, East might well have asked for a spade return anyway to kill dummy's spades, but if not, the possibility of discards on dummy's spades makes it imperative to take your heart tricks quickly. A trump return cannot achieve that. A heart to the ace, heart to the king and a third heart would take 3 ◇ two off.

Note that in 1♠ doubled, if North leads a diamond to the ace and a diamond is returned, West can score a heart ruff in dummy and make the contract! Lest you think that this makes the 1♠ overcall a smart move, N-S at the other table bid to 4♠, West doubled and that was minus 500.

Trump Lead?

A trump lead can be part of a definite plan of attack (to cut down ruffs in dummy or to minimise declarer's cross-ruff) or simply a passive lead to avoid presenting a trick to declarer with some other lead. There are times, though, when a trump lead can be downright risky. The situations when a trump lead is to be avoided are covered by **F.U.N.D.S.**

Stay away from a trump lead if any of these features exist:

F.	You hold	Four or more trumps (see **TLLL** below)
U.	There is a	Useful suit in dummy (see **DILLUS**, pages 63-64)
N.	There was	No support shown by dummy
D.	You have a	Dangerous trump holding from which to lead
S.	You have a	Singleton trump

Four or more trumps

When you hold four or more trumps, there is a general strategy that should usually be adopted. Try this problem:

Dealer South : Both vulnerable

WEST	NORTH	EAST	SOUTH
			1♡
No	2♣	No	3♣
No	3♡	No	4♡
No	No	No	

What should West lead from:

♠ 9 7 3   ♡ A K Q 2   ◇ Q 9 8 3 2   ♣ 2

T.L.L.L.
True Love Lasts Longest

When you have four or more trumps, you are a powerful thorn in declarer's side. Declarer has to use up most of his trumps to remove yours and may not be able to afford that. In general, with four or more trumps, do not lead a trump and do not lead a singleton (but exceptions exist). If you lead a singleton and score a ruff, you have reduced your trump length and pose less of a threat. With 4+ trumps, follow **TLLL**:

T.	**T**rump	**T**rue
L.	**L**ength,	**L**ove
L.	**L**ead	**L**asts
L.	**L**ength	**L**ongest

With long trumps your aim is to force declarer to ruff and so reduce declarer's trump length. If you have four trumps and declarer has five, declarer will be down to four trumps, the same as you, if declarer has to ruff once. If you can force declarer to ruff twice, declarer has only three trumps left. With more trumps, you should be able to control the flow of the play. Declarer has 'lost control'.

This approach, known as a 'forcing defence', is particularly satisfying when it works. If you want to make declarer ruff, which suit offers you the best chance? Your longest suit, naturally. Hence, follow **T.L.L.L.** — **T**rump **L**ength, **L**ead **L**ength. You should adopt the same approach when the bidding tells you that partner is likely to have trump length.

TLLL provides the solution to that opening lead problem:

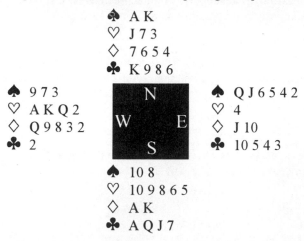

♠ A K
♡ J 7 3
◇ 7 6 5 4
♣ K 9 8 6

♠ 9 7 3
♡ A K Q 2
◇ Q 9 8 3 2
♣ 2

♠ Q J 6 5 4 2
♡ 4
◇ J 10
♣ 10 5 4 3

♠ 10 8
♡ 10 9 8 6 5
◇ A K
♣ A Q J 7

On a trump, club or spade lead, declarer simply leads trumps at every opportunity and loses just three tricks. On a diamond lead, East plays the 10 (**LOEITS** — see page 37). South wins and leads a trump. West wins and continues diamonds. South wins and leads another trump. A third diamond forces South to ruff and now declarer is doomed. Another trump will lead to two down. If trumps are abandoned, West ruffs a club.

Useful long suit in dummy

Where dummy has a long suit, leading a trump plays straight into declarer's hand. Review **DILLUS** (pages 62-67) if you have doubts here.

No support shown by dummy

A trump lead is likely to work best if dummy has raised declarer's suit. If dummy has shown no support, a trump lead may trap partner's honour holding. After they bid 1♠ : 2◇, 4♠ a trump lead is not a good idea.

♠ - - -

♠ 6 5 2   ♠ K J 3

♠ A Q 10 9 8 7 4

Declarer has two trump losers unless West kindly leads a trump and reduces declarer's losers to one. Partner *will* be displeased. For a dramatic example of the danger in leading a trump here, see **H.U.R.T.** at page 90.

Dangerous trump holding

A trump lead from an unsupported honour such as K-x, Q-x-x, J-x-x-x is risky and similarly from honour combinations such as A-J-x, A-10-x.

Singleton trump

If you have a singleton trump partner is likely to have three or four. Leading a trump may destroy a potential winner for partner. Witness:

A 7 3 2

You: 4   Q 10 8

K J 9 6 5

With no clues, declarer is likely to play ace and king and lose a trick. Lead your singleton and declarer will say 'Thank *you* very much.'

K 6 2

You: 4   J 10 8 5

A Q 9 7 3

Similarly, declarer's normal play is ace and low to the king. If so, partner makes a trick. Lead your singleton and declarer plays low from dummy and captures partner's honour. Low to the king now reveals the position, enabling declarer to finesse the 9 and capture partner's other honour. *There are a number of ways to irritate your partner but leading a singleton trump is one of the most effective.*

70

Follow Trump Leads From The '90s
(T.T.T.T.T.T.T.T.T)

As long as **FUNDS** has not excluded a trump lead, you will be in front more often if you follow the nine **Ts** for trump leads.

A trump lead is worth strong consideration in these situations:

T.		Try a trump if out of **FUNDS** and others worse
T.	There is a	Two-suiter shown by declarer or dummy.
T.	There is a	Three-suiter shown by declarer or dummy.
T.	Their	Third bid suit has become the trump suit.
T.	They are	Too high for their expected point count.
T.	There are	Three suits where your side is strong outside trumps.
T.	They are	Taking a sacrifice.
T.	Your	Takeout double at the 1-level was passed by partner.
T.	There is a	Twin fit (4-4 or 4-3) and you have 5 low trumps.

Try a trump if out of FUNDS

If **FUNDS** does not apply and you have no attractive lead, try a trump.

Two-suiter shown by declarer or dummy

W	E	
1♠	1NT	West has shown a two-suiter and dummy preferred the second suit. Clearly dummy has more cards in the second suit. Losers in declarer's first suit can be ruffed.
2♦	No	

To cut down the ruffs, you should lead a trump, particularly if you are strong in declarer's first suit.

W	N	E	S	
1♠	2NT	No	3♦	Dummy has shown a two-suiter and declarer chose diamonds. South probably has more diamonds than clubs. Dummy's club suit might be set up by ruffing in declarer's hand.
No	No	No		

To cut down the ruffs, you should lead a trump, particularly if you are strong in clubs.

Three-suiter shown by declarer or dummy

When declarer or dummy has shown a three-suiter (4-4-4-1 or 5-4-4-0 pattern), the hand is often played as a cross-ruff. The best defence against a cross-ruff is trump leads at every opportunity.

Third bid suit has become the trump suit

W	E	When their third suit becomes the trump suit, dummy
1♠	2◇	is often short in declarer's first suit and declarer is likely
2♡	4♡	to be short in dummy's suit. How does declarer play
No		such a hand? As a cross-ruff is imminent, lead trumps.

Too high for their point count

If the opponents are bidding beyond the level suggested by their point count, how do they expect to succeed? As they cannot hope to make the contract with their high cards, they must be counting on scoring the extra trick(s) by ruffs. Reduce that option by leading trumps.

Three suits where your side is strong outside trumps

If your side is known to be strong in three suits, the tricks in those suits will come to you as long as they are not ruffed away. Lead a trump in order to protect your strength.

Taking a sacrifice

If they are sacrificing against your contract, by definition they are bidding beyond their high card values. It is also very likely that your side is strong in three suits and that declarer may play the hand as a cross-ruff. All these factors point strongly to a trump lead. Against a sacrifice, a trump lead may be justified even with a singleton trump or from a dangerous trump holding such as Q-x-x.

Takeout double at the 1-level passed by partner

W	N	E	S	Partner passes your takeout double only with
1◇	Dble	No	No	better trumps than declarer. You should lead
No				a trump, even a singleton, to enable partner to
				draw declarer's trumps.

Twin fit (4-4 or 4-3) and you have 5 low trumps

If they are in a 4-3 or 4-4 fit and you have five low trumps, they are in serious jeopardy. To cut down the opportunity for declarer scoring the trumps separately, lead a trump and draw two for one every time you are on lead. This is an exception to the **Trump Length, Lead Length** rule (see pages 68-69).

Singleton lead?

W.H.A.T. Makes A Good Singleton Lead

WEST	NORTH	EAST	SOUTH
1♠	No	3♠	No
4♠	No	No	No

What should North lead from each of these hands?

1. ♠ 4 3 2	2. ♠ 4 3 2	3. ♠ A 3 2
♡ 7	♡ 7	♡ 7
◇ K Q 8 4 2	◇ 8 6 4 3 2	◇ 8 6 4 3 2
♣ A Q J 7	♣ A Q 6 5	♣ 10 9 5 3

For a singleton lead to work, two things need to happen. Partner must be able to gain the lead in order to lead back the suit you can ruff and that has to occur before declarer is able to draw your trumps. To maximise the chances of a successful singleton lead, consider **W.H.A.T.**

W.	**W**eak	A weak hand is a strong indication that a
H.	**H**and,	singleton lead is attractive.
A.	**A**ce of	Holding A-x or A-x-x in trumps is also a
T.	**T**rumps	strong suggestion in favour of a singleton lead.

If you have a weak hand, partner is likely to have a strong hand and thus the entries needed to give you one or two ruffs. The weaker the hand, the more probable that a singleton lead will turn out well. (The same holds for a doubleton lead: the weaker your hand, the better.)

If you have the trump ace, declarer cannot draw your trumps instantly. Even if partner lacks the ace in the suit you lead, you have another chance of finding partner's entry after you come in with the trump ace. (Similarly, K-x-x is a good trump holding for a singleton lead.) The best combination is a weak hand with the ace of trumps, eh **WHAT**?

#1: Lead the ◇K. You are too strong for the heart lead. Partner is unlikely to hold a quick entry.

#2: A singleton lead is reasonable but may prove futile if declarer draws your trumps. A trump lead is not a bad shot. Not suspecting a shortage, declarer may lead hearts and you score your ruff after all.

#3: Ideal for the singleton heart lead.

CHAPTER 7

MNEMONICS FOR DECLARER & DEFENDERS

The JFK Principle

1. Dealer North : Nil vulnerable

     ♠ J 8 4
     ♡ J 7 5 4
     ◊ Q J 6
     ♣ K J 6

       ♠ 9 5
       ♡ 6 2
       ◊ A 7 5 3 2
       ♣ 9 8 3 2

WEST	NORTH	EAST	SOUTH
	No	No	1♡
No	2♡	No	4♡
No	No	No	

West starts with the ace of spades and continues with the king and queen of spades. How do you ensure a diamond switch at trick 4?

2. Dealer South : Nil vulnerable

     ♠ J 8 4 3 2
     ♡ J
     ◊ Q J 6 4 2
     ♣ J 6

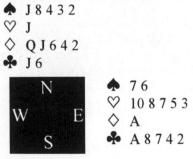

       ♠ 7 6
       ♡ 10 8 7 5 3
       ◊ A
       ♣ A 8 7 4 2

South opens 1♠ and North's jump to 4♠ ends proceedings. West leads the king of clubs. How do you plan the defence?

1.

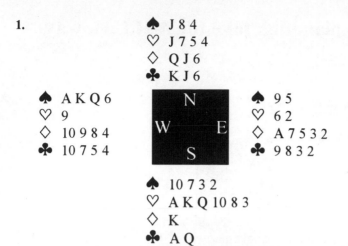

♠ J 8 4
♡ J 7 5 4
◇ Q J 6
♣ K J 6

♠ A K Q 6
♡ 9
◇ 10 9 8 4
♣ 10 7 5 4

♠ 9 5
♡ 6 2
◇ A 7 5 3 2
♣ 9 8 3 2

♠ 10 7 3 2
♡ A K Q 10 8 3
◇ K
♣ A Q

Against 4♡, West starts with three rounds of spades. To make sure of the diamond switch, East ruffs the third spade and cashes the ◇ A.

No doubt John F. Kennedy had bridge players in mind when he said:

> *'Ask not what your (partner) can do for you,*
> *ask what you can do for (yourself).'*

If you know what must be done, heed **JFK** and do it yourself.

2.

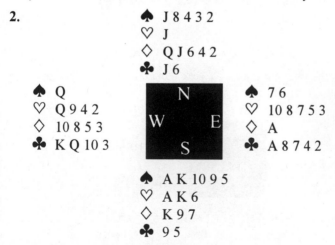

♠ J 8 4 3 2
♡ J
◇ Q J 6 4 2
♣ J 6

♠ Q
♡ Q 9 4 2
◇ 10 8 5 3
♣ K Q 10 3

♠ 7 6
♡ 10 8 7 5 3
◇ A
♣ A 8 7 4 2

♠ A K 10 9 5
♡ A K 6
◇ K 9 7
♣ 9 5

West leads the ♣K against 4♠. Heeding **JFK**, East overtakes with the ♣A, cashes ◇A and returns a club. The diamond ruff beats the contract.

For planning, take the A.R.C.H. way

1.

                ♠ A K 4
                ♡ K J 6
                ◇ Q J 2
                ♣ Q 7 6 4

                        ♠ Q 9 5
                        ♡ A Q 4 3
                        ◇ 8 7 5
                        ♣ 9 8 3

South opens 1NT (12-14) and North bids 3NT. West leads the 2 of spades, 4 from dummy and your queen wins. How should you continue?

2.
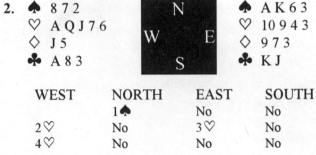

♠ 8 7 2   ♠ A K 6 3
♡ A Q J 7 6   ♡ 10 9 4 3
◇ J 5   ◇ 9 7 3
♣ A 8 3   ♣ K J

WEST	NORTH	EAST	SOUTH
	1♠	No	No
2♡	No	3♡	No
4♡	No	No	No

North leads the ♣2 and dummy's jack wins the trick. A 1NT opening by North-South would be 12-14 balanced. Plan the play.

3.
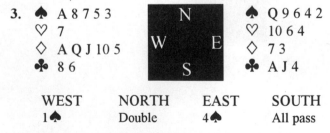

♠ A 8 7 5 3   ♠ Q 9 6 4 2
♡ 7   ♡ 10 6 4
◇ A Q J 10 5   ◇ 7 3
♣ 8 6   ♣ A J 4

WEST	NORTH	EAST	SOUTH
1♠	Double	4♠	All pass

North leads the ♡K, which holds, and after a little thought continues with the 3 of hearts to South's ace which you ruff. Plan the play from here.

I first came across A.R.C.H. in a George Gooden Beginners' Book and found it a very sensible plan to follow as soon as dummy comes into view.

A.   **A**nalyse the opening lead
R.   **R**eview the bidding
C.   **C**ount . . .
H.   **H**ow should I plan the play?

A: Was the lead fourth-highest? What does that tell you about the length held by the opening leader? Was it an honour card lead? What does that promise or deny?

R: What can you tell about the opponents' hands from their bidding? Even the failure to bid carries information.

C: Count your instant tricks in no-trumps, your losers in a trump contract and count the HCP in dummy whatever the contract. In a trump contract it also makes sense to count your winners if they are obvious.

In no-trumps if your instant winners are fewer than needed, you normally start on the suit that can bring in the extra tricks.

In a trump contract with more losers than you can afford, can the excess losers be eliminated by ruffing? By discarding? This may entail delaying trumps or creating extra winners in dummy on which to pitch losers.

By counting dummy's HCP and adding your own, you can tell how many HCP are in the other two hands (by deducting the total from 40). Often you can make a close estimate of how many points are in each of the unseen hands. Counting the visible HCP is such a valuable data bank, it should become an unshakable habit the moment dummy appears.

A.R.C.H. was intended for declarer but a defender can benefit from the same approach. Just as declarer has a goal, so a defender should consider the tricks needed to defeat declarer as the defensive contract.

If you are defending, you can usually estimate declarer's HCP within a couple of points and that in turn will indicate how many points your partner can hold. Knowing partner's possible strength can save you from embarking on a futile defence. I am surprised, and dismayed, at how many players do not bother to make use of this little gem.

H: After Analyse, Review and Count, you often have a good idea of the problems in the hand and that may point the way to overcoming them. **A.R.C.H.** is a useful drill that should be applied hand after hand.

You may now wish to review your answers to Problems 1-3.

1.

♠ A K 4
♡ K J 6
◇ Q J 2
♣ Q 7 6 4

♠ 10 7 3 2
♡ 8 7 2
◇ 9 6 4
♣ A 10 5

♠ Q 9 5
♡ A Q 4 3
◇ 8 7 5
♣ 9 8 3

♠ J 8 6
♡ 10 9 5
◇ A K 10 3
♣ K J 2

Against 3NT West leads the 2 of spades, ducked to East's queen.

Analyse the lead: The ♠2, 4th-highest, indicates a 4-card suit only.

Review the bidding: South's 1NT showed 12-14 points.

Count the HCP: Dummy has 16 HCP, you have 8. Total: 24. South's 12-14 brings the total to 36-38. Therefore partner has 2-4 points. As it happens, all the queens are visible so that if partner has 2 points, it would be two jacks, which would be useless.

If partner has 3 or 4 points, partner will have a minor suit king or ace. If you return a spade, declarer is very likely to knock out partner's high card next to establish extra tricks in that minor. Partner will then have no entry to enjoy the 13th spade later.

Count the tricks: You have one spade trick and hope that partner will win a trick in a minor. Adding two for the ♡A-Q comes to four tricks. The only chance for a fifth trick is from your length card in hearts.

How will you achieve that? After taking the queen of spades, you should switch to the 3 of hearts. On winning with the ace of clubs, partner needs to cooperate by returning a heart but that should be clear from the line of defence you have chosen. Would you have found this defence without counting the points in dummy?

3NT can make (rise with ♠A and play on clubs) but that is not your concern, and ducking the spade was certainly a reasonable play.

2.

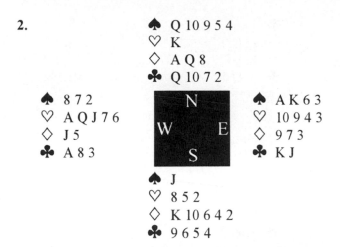

♠ Q 10 9 5 4
♡ K
◇ A Q 8
♣ Q 10 7 2

♠ 8 7 2
♡ A Q J 7 6
◇ J 5
♣ A 8 3

♠ A K 6 3
♡ 10 9 4 3
◇ 9 7 3
♣ K J

♠ J
♡ 8 5 2
◇ K 10 6 4 2
♣ 9 6 5 4

Against 4♡ (passing 3♡ might have been more prudent), North leads the 2 of clubs and dummy's jack wins.

Analyse the lead: The ♣2 indicates a 4-card suit or perhaps bottom from Q-x-x only. More important than the lead chosen are the leads that were not chosen. As Q-x-x or Q-x-x-x is not a very appealing choice, ask yourself why North did not lead a diamond. If North's diamonds were headed by the A-K, that would be a standout choice and K-Q of diamonds would also appeal more than leading away from the ♣Q. You can therefore place South with the ◇K.

Review the bidding: North opened 1♠ and South passed (0-5 points).

Count the HCP: Dummy has 11 HCP, you have 12. Total: 23. The opponents began with 17. You have placed South with 3 points (◇K). With 12-14 balanced, North would have opened 1NT. As North cannot hold more than 14 and did not open 1NT, North figures to have five spades. With spades headed by Q-J-9 / Q-J-10, North would have led a spade. Therefore you can also place South with the ♠J. As South passed 1♠, South cannot have the ♡K in addition to the ◇K (and ♠J).

Count the losers: 2 in diamonds, 1 in spades, perhaps 1 in hearts.

How will you play? Since the ♡K is marked with North, reject the heart finesse. Play the ♡A and hope the king is singleton.

3.

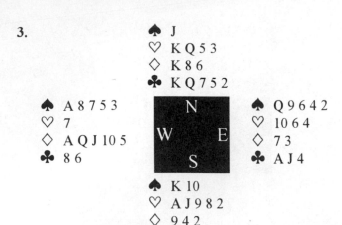

```
            ♠ J
            ♡ K Q 5 3
            ◇ K 8 6
            ♣ K Q 7 5 2
♠ A 8 7 5 3                    ♠ Q 9 6 4 2
♡ 7                           ♡ 10 6 4
◇ A Q J 10 5                  ◇ 7 3
♣ 8 6                         ♣ A J 4
            ♠ K 10
            ♡ A J 9 8 2
            ◇ 9 4 2
            ♣ 10 9 3
```

Against 4♠, North leads ♡K, then ♡3. You ruff South's ace.

Analyse the lead: North has led from ♡K-Q and South began with ♡A-J. If North had started with ♡K-Q-J-x, North would continue with ♡Q rather than ♡3.

Review the bidding: North's takeout double suggests shortage in spades and 3+ cards in each other suit, usually with 12+ HCP.

Count the losers: You have lost one heart and have a loser in clubs. There may also be a spade loser and a diamond loser. As you have no choice in the play of the spades, you cash the ♠A. When the king does not drop, you do have a trump loser.

Count the HCP: You have 11, dummy has 7. Total 18. They began with 22 HCP. You have placed South with ♡A-J and it is slightly more likely that South has the ♠K (because of North's takeout double). That would give South 8 HCP and so almost all the others will be with North including the ◇K. Should you finesse South for the ◇K or is there some other way to reduce your losers to three?

How will you play? After ♠A, lead the ◇10. North might well duck with the ◇K and then you have no diamond loser. If South has the ◇K, North will probably have the ♠K and you should be able to discard two clubs from dummy on the diamonds before North ruffs. If North does take the ◇K and shifts to a club, take the ♣A and run diamonds, discarding clubs. You have to hope that the player with the ♠K holds at least three diamonds.

H.U.R.T.

1.  ♠ J 7 6
   ♡ A J 10 6 4 3
   ◇ K J 7
   ♣ K

   ♠ 10 5 3 2
   ♡ K 2
   ◇ A Q 10
   ♣ A 6 4 3

After 1NT by East, 4♡ from West, the defenders cash three spades (all follow) and shift to a club. You take ♣K, play a heart to the king and finesse the ♡J. There is good news and bad news. The heart finesse wins but North shows out. South has ♡Q-x left. How do you play from here?

2. ♠ Q J 9 8 6 3
   ♡ 5
   ◇ 8 6 4
   ♣ A 5 3

   ♠ A K
   ♡ A K Q J
   ◇ Q 7 3 2
   ♣ K Q 6

WEST	NORTH	EAST	SOUTH
2♠ (1)	No	2NT (2)	No
3♣ (3)	No	4♠	All pass

(1) Weak two   (2) Enquiry   (3) Minimum hand, weak suit

North leads the ◇9 and South wins with ◇10. South cashes ◇K, ◇5 from North, and the ◇A, North pitching a club. South continues with the ◇J and as you ruff with the ♠J, you notice a triumphant smile from South. North discards another club. When you cash ♠A, ♠K, North discards on the second spade and South still has the ♠10-7 left while you hold ♠Q-9-8. Will you be able to wipe the smile off South's face?

3. ♠ A Q J 8 6 3
   ♡ 5
   ◇ A K 5
   ♣ A 4 2

   ♠ 10 5
   ♡ A 9 8 7 3
   ◇ 7 3 2
   ♣ K Q J

Against your 6♠, North starts with the 10 of diamonds. You win with the ace, play a club to dummy and run the 10 of spades. It wins. You continue with a spade to your queen which wins but North discards a diamond. South still has ♠K-9. How do you play from here?

When you strike a trump position where you cannot catch a missing trump honour, there is a technique which may lead to success by nullifying the enemy trumps. The key element in this technique is to reduce your trumps to the same length as your opponent. For example:

5

You	Dummy
K 10 7 4 3 2	A Q

J 9 8 6

When you play the ace and queen, North shows out and South has the uncatchable J-9. To trap South's trumps, you need to ruff twice to bring your trump length down to the same number as South's. Once you have done that, the lead must not be in your own hand at trick 12. That is the message of **H.U.R.T.**

H.	<u>H</u>onour(s)	If you follow this approach and thus make
U.	<u>U</u>ncatchable,	your contract, the opponents will be the
R.	<u>R</u>educe	ones hurt instead of you. You may now wish
T.	<u>T</u>rumps	to review problems 1-3 before reading on.

1.

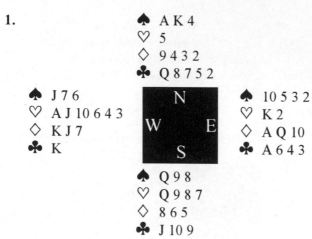

♠ A K 4
♡ 5
◇ 9 4 3 2
♣ Q 8 7 5 2

♠ J 7 6
♡ A J 10 6 4 3
◇ K J 7
♣ K

♠ 10 5 3 2
♡ K 2
◇ A Q 10
♣ A 6 4 3

♠ Q 9 8
♡ Q 9 8 7
◇ 8 6 5
♣ J 10 9

Against 4♡, the defence starts with three rounds of spades and South shifts to a club. You take the ♣K, cross to ♡K and take the heart finesse, North showing out. That hurts but **H.U.R.T.** saves you. Cross to the ◇10, ruff a club, cross to the ◇Q, ruff a club, leaving this ending:

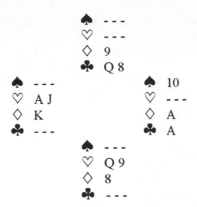

Cross to the ◇A and on either card from dummy, South's trump 'winner' evaporates. Three diamond entries to dummy are needed. If South held 0-2 diamonds, you would fail. You must not shorten your trumps by leading the thirteenth spade from dummy. That would allow South to discard a diamond and you could not return to dummy in diamonds at trick 11.

If South switches to diamonds at trick 4, win ◇10, cash ♡K and take the heart finesse. Now overtake ♣K with ♣A, ruff a club, diamond to the queen, ruff a club, and a diamond to the ace produces the same result.

2.

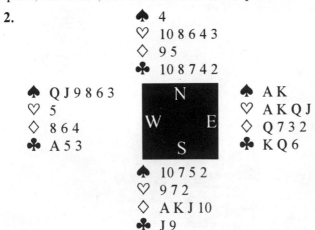

Against 4♠, you sensibly ruff the fourth diamond high. ♠A, ♠K reveal the bad news. Play a heart to dummy and ruff a heart to reduce your trumps to the same length as South's. Lead a club to dummy and continue hearts, discarding clubs. South is not smiling any more!

On the preceding two hands, you finished in dummy at trick 12. While this is common enough for trump reduction plays, it is not essential. What is vital is that you are not in your own hand at trick 12:

3.

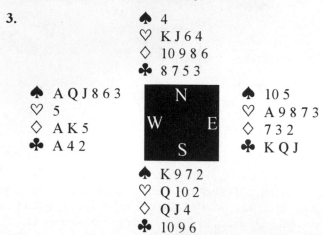

♠ 4
♡ K J 6 4
◇ 10 9 8 6
♣ 8 7 5 3

♠ A Q J 8 6 3
♡ 5
◇ A K 5
♣ A 4 2

♠ 10 5
♡ A 9 8 7 3
◇ 7 3 2
♣ K Q J

♠ K 9 7 2
♡ Q 10 2
◇ Q J 4
♣ 10 9 6

Against your pushy 6♠, North leads the ◇10. After a club to dummy, you run the ♠10, which wins. A spade to the queen follows but North shows out. Enter **H.U.R.T.** Heart to the ace, ruff a heart, club to dummy, ruff a heart. Trump reduction complete. Now cash ♣A and ◇A (if South ruffs either of these you were always doomed) and exit with the third diamond. You are left with ♠A-J and no matter who wins the third diamond, the last two tricks are yours.

Love **HURT**s? Good. Now try these problems.

4. Dealer West : North-South vulnerable

♠ 8 7 5
♡ K 10 9 5 4 3
◇ 3
♣ A K J

♠ J 4 3
♡ A Q
◇ A 8 7 5 2
♣ Q 9 3

Against silent opposition, you reach 4♡ and the defence starts with three rounds of spades, followed by a club switch.
How do you plan the play?

5. Dealer West : Nil vulnerable

♠ 8	♠ A 10 7
♡ K 9 7 4 3 2	♡ Q J 5
◇ K Q 7	◇ A J 5 3
♣ A K 3	♣ Q 9 7

West is in 6♡ with North-South silent. The ♠K is led. Plan the play.

6. Dealer West : Nil vulnerable

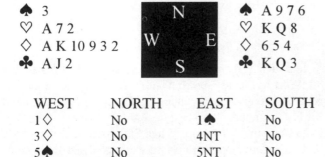

♠ Q 2	♠ A K 10 9 7
♡ 10 9	♡ K 8 7 3
◇ 3	◇ K J 2
♣ A J 8 7 6 5 3 2	♣ K

Against West's 3♣, the ♡Q is led, king, ace. South returns ♡5 to North's jack and after cashing ◇A, North continues with the ♡6, ♡8 from dummy, and South follows with the ♡2. Plan the play from here.

7. Dealer West : North-South vulnerable

♠ 3	♠ A 9 7 6
♡ A 7 2	♡ K Q 8
◇ A K 10 9 3 2	◇ 6 5 4
♣ A J 2	♣ K Q 3

WEST	NORTH	EAST	SOUTH
1◇	No	1♠	No
3◇	No	4NT	No
5♠	No	5NT	No
6◇	No	No	No

North leads the ♡J taken in dummy. On any normal split in diamonds, this would be child's play but when you lead the ◇4 from dummy, South discards the ♠8. Can you survive this vile break?

8. Dealer South : East-West vulnerable

♠ A 10 2	**N**	♠ K Q 7
♡ Q 4	**W E**	♡ A 10 9 3 2
◇ K Q		◇ A 10 7 5
♣ A K Q 9 8 4	**S**	♣ 7

On a sequence you do not care to have published, you have reached 7♣ with no opposition bidding. North leads the two of clubs to South's 10 and your ace. When you cash the king of clubs, North plays the ♣3 and South the ♣5. How would you continue?

Solutions

4.

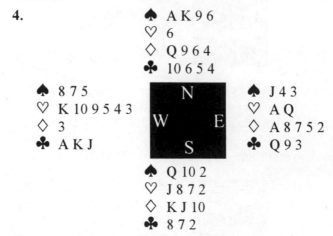

	♠ A K 9 6	
	♡ 6	
	◇ Q 9 6 4	
	♣ 10 6 5 4	
♠ 8 7 5	**N**	♠ J 4 3
♡ K 10 9 5 4 3	**W E**	♡ A Q
◇ 3		◇ A 8 7 5 2
♣ A K J	**S**	♣ Q 9 3
	♠ Q 10 2	
	♡ J 8 7 2	
	◇ K J 10	
	♣ 8 7 2	

West is in 4♡ and after three rounds of spades, South shifts to a club. If hearts are 3-2, West has it easy, but if South has ♡J-x-x-x, **H.U.R.T.** will help provided that you start soon enough. At trick 5 play a diamond to the ace and ruff a diamond. Then cash ♡A, ♡Q. If trumps are 3-2, return to hand and draw the last trump. When South still has ♡J-x, ruff another diamond to reduce your trumps once more. Then cash clubs ending in dummy at trick 11 and all is well.

Note that the paucity of entries to dummy means that you must start the trump reduction before you know the trump split. If you play ♡A, ♡Q and then ◇A, diamond ruff, club to the queen and diamond ruff, you have shortened your trumps but you cannot return to dummy. Doom!

5.

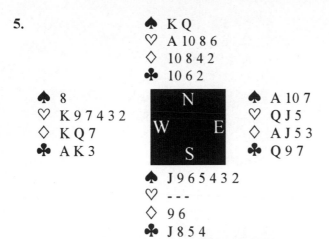

       ♠ K Q
       ♡ A 10 8 6
       ◇ 10 8 4 2
       ♣ 10 6 2

♠ 8   ♠ A 10 7
♡ K 9 7 4 3 2   ♡ Q J 5
◇ K Q 7   ◇ A J 5 3
♣ A K 3   ♣ Q 9 7

       ♠ J 9 6 5 4 3 2
       ♡ - - -
       ◇ 9 6
       ♣ J 8 5 4

The same principle is at work on this deal from a 1997 U.K. county match reported by Freddie North. West is in 6♡ against silent opponents and North leads the ♠K. Declarer took the ♠A and led the ♡Q . . . curtains. Since the contract is almost certain on a 2-2 or 3-1 heart split and you can easily deal with ♡A-10-8-6 with South, the only possible problem is when North holds all four trumps.

To cater for that, use **H.U.R.T.** As North's trump honours are uncatchable, start reducing trumps at once. If you succeed, you will have a brilliancy to cherish for the rest of your days. The winning line: ruff a spade at trick 2 and lead a trump. North must play low and dummy's queen wins. Three rounds of diamonds follow, ending in dummy and since North began with four diamonds, ruff dummy's last diamond rather than a spade. Then cash ♣A, ♣K and play a club to the queen to leave this position:

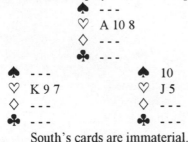

       ♠ - - -
       ♡ A 10 8
       ◇ - - -
       ♣ - - -

♠ - - -   ♠ 10
♡ K 9 7   ♡ J 5
◇ - - -   ◇ - - -
♣ - - -   ♣ - - -

    South's cards are immaterial.

You lead the ♠10 from dummy and ruff with the ♡K. North is without recourse and can score only the ace of trumps. Doesn't that feel great?

6.

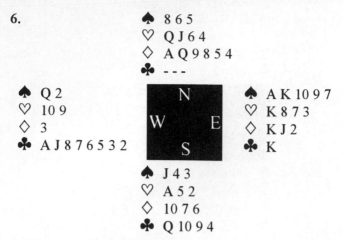

```
              ♠ 8 6 5
              ♡ Q J 6 4
              ◇ A Q 9 8 5 4
              ♣ - - -
♠ Q 2                         ♠ A K 10 9 7
♡ 10 9          N            ♡ K 8 7 3
◇ 3         W       E        ◇ K J 2
♣ A J 8 7 6 5 3 2   S        ♣ K
              ♠ J 4 3
              ♡ A 5 2
              ◇ 10 7 6
              ♣ Q 10 9 4
```

In the 1997 Australian Autumn National Teams, Rob Buttrose applied **H.U.R.T.** to land 3♣ despite the 4-0 split. North led ♡Q, king, ace, and won the heart return. He cashed ◇A and played a third heart, hoping South might ruff. Some might discard a spade on the ♡8 but Buttrose did the right thing. He ruffed. If trumps were 4-0, trump reduction could be vital.

A club to the king revealed the bad break. Declarer continued his trump reduction via ◇J ruffed, ♠2 to the king, ◇K (another winner) ruffed, ♠Q overtaking with ♠A and a spade ruff. This was the end-position:

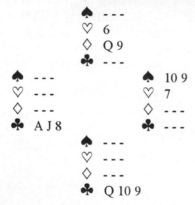

```
              ♠ - - -
              ♡ 6
              ◇ Q 9
              ♣ - - -
♠ - - -                   ♠ 10 9
♡ - - -                   ♡ 7
◇ - - -                   ◇ - - -
♣ A J 8                   ♣ - - -
              ♠ - - -
              ♡ - - -
              ◇ - - -
              ♣ Q 10 9
```

Declarer exited with the 8 of clubs and claimed the last two tricks. Ruffing the heart at trick 4 was essential. If West had four clubs left in the ending, South would have a spare card and the contract would fail.

7.

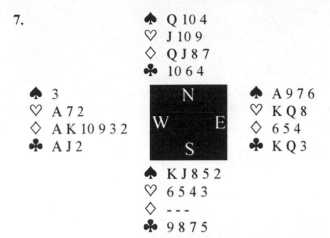

♠ Q 10 4
♥ J 10 9
♦ Q J 8 7
♣ 10 6 4

♠ 3
♥ A 7 2
♦ A K 10 9 3 2
♣ A J 2

♠ A 9 7 6
♥ K Q 8
♦ 6 5 4
♣ K Q 3

♠ K J 8 5 2
♥ 6 5 4 3
♦ - - -
♣ 9 8 7 5

Luck and **H.U.R.T.** technique may overcome seemingly insurmountable obstacles. On seeing dummy, North 'knew' he had two trump tricks against 6 ♦. West demonstrated that all is not what it seems.

The ♥J lead was won in dummy and South's ♠8 discard on the ♦4 revealed the trump break. With a **H.U.R.T.** look on his face, West continued with a spade to the ace and a spade ruff, followed by a club to the king and another spade ruff. So far, so good. West still needed some luck, namely that North would not be able to ruff in on the hearts or the clubs.

After cashing all the winners outside trumps without mishap, declarer reached this ending:

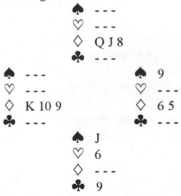

♠ - - -
♥ - - -
♦ Q J 8
♣ - - -

♠ - - -
♥ - - -
♦ K 10 9
♣ - - -

♠ 9
♥ - - -
♦ 6 5
♣ - - -

♠ J
♥ 6
♦ - - -
♣ 9

The ♦9 gave North a trump trick but declarer made the last two.

8.

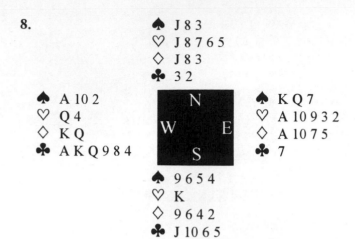

```
                ♠ J 8 3
                ♡ J 8 7 6 5
                ◇ J 8 3
                ♣ 3 2
♠ A 10 2          N          ♠ K Q 7
♡ Q 4                        ♡ A 10 9 3 2
◇ K Q        W       E       ◇ A 10 7 5
♣ A K Q 9 8 4     S          ♣ 7
                ♠ 9 6 5 4
                ♡ K
                ◇ 9 6 4 2
                ♣ J 10 6 5
```

In Indonesia v Hong Kong in the 1997 Pacific Asian Open Teams, Indonesia bid and made 6NT. At the other table, Roger Ling of Hong Kong reached 7♣ from the West seat. North led the ♣2 and South played the ♣10 (a falsecard with the jack might have been better). Declarer drew a second round of trumps and considered the situation.

North's low-high lead in trumps suggested a doubleton (middle-down-up is normal with three rags) and so Ling decided to play South to have started with ♣J-10-x-x. That would mean South had ♣J-x left and so Ling set about a trump reduction.

The king and queen of diamonds were cashed, followed by the ♡4 to the ace. When South's ♡K fell, the ♡Q was high but declarer promptly disposed of that winner on the ace of diamonds. A diamond was ruffed, followed by a spade to the king and a heart ruff. That brought West down to ♣Q-9, the same length as South's ♣J-6.

Declarer concluded the coup with the ace of spades and a spade to dummy. A heart from dummy at trick 12 picked off South's trumps. Ooohh, that **H.U.R.T**.

CHAPTER 8

VISUALISATION, IMAGERY & MNEMONICS

One of the reasons that mnemonics work so well is that visual recall is much stronger than verbal recall. You should be able to improve the efficacy of the bridge mnemonics by conjuring up a vision of each mnemonic including the bridge principle involved somewhere within the picture you have visualised. The more absurd the image the better since the memory imprint will then be more powerful.

For example, for **S.S.S.A.P.** (**S**oftly, **S**oftly, **S**aints **A**t **P**rayer) you might imagine a group of saints on their knees praying with the balloon above them reading 'Please Lord, give me a **S**hort, **S**trong **S**uit to lead'.

For **R.T.T.** (**R**aise **T**he **T**itanic) you might see the mighty ship just coming up out of the water and on the side is scrawled the combination of K-10-x-x opposite A-Q-x-x with **R**etain **T**he **T**enace written below.

M.A.F.I.A. can be seen as an army parade with the ones at the front all being majors (**MA**jors **FI**rst **A**lways).

A.R.C.H. is easy to visualise as the Arc de Triomphe with the principles in huge letters on the monument, **A**nalyse the lead, **R**eview the bidding, **C**ount the tricks, the losers, the points, and **H**ow do I make this contract?

Some of them may tax your ingenuity and your visualisation may be more creative than mine. For **DILL US?**, how about a gigantic baby's dummy (**D**ummy **I**s **L**ong) holding on to a leash and on the other end of the leash is a man's suit with a sign on it, 'Failed to meet reserve price,' (**L**ead **U**nbid **S**uit)?

H.U.R.T. (**H**onours **U**ncatchable, **R**educe **T**rumps) could be a group of judges fleeing, escaping over a border, and the captain of the pursuing army shouting to his trumpeters, 'Reduce Trumps!'

I will leave the others, including **S. & M. to inflict pain**, to your own vivid imagination. You might then consider what visions you can produce to solve this final set of problems.

1. Dealer West : Nil vulnerable

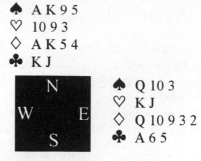

♠ A K 9 5
♥ 10 9 3
♦ A K 5 4
♣ K J

♠ Q 10 3
♥ K J
♦ Q 10 9 3 2
♣ A 6 5

WEST	NORTH	EAST	SOUTH
No	1♦	No	1♠
No	2NT	No	3♥
No	4♠	No	5♦ - - - cue-bid
No	5♠	All pass	

West leads the ♣10: king – ace – 2. How should East continue?

This is a good hand for **A.R.C.H.**

Analyse the lead: The ♣10 lead is from a 10-9 sequence. The ♣10 could be from a Q-10-9 suit but that is refuted by declarer's play of the ♣K from dummy. Lacking the ♣Q, declarer would play dummy's ♣J (since the opening lead of a low club almost certainly denies holding the ace).

Review the bidding: South's first two bids show at least 5-4 in the majors. That means that South has at most four cards in the minors. South has made a slam try and the cue-bid in diamonds is virtually certain to be a void.

Count the HCP: Dummy has 18 HCP, you have 12. Total: 30. If South is void in diamonds, South must have the remaining 9 HCP (♠J, ♥A-Q and ♣Q) to justify the slam try.

Count the tricks: You have a club trick in and one trump trick to come. There can be no more tricks in the minors. The only hope for another trick is in hearts.

How can you hope to score a heart trick if declarer has the A-Q?

Your best chance is to shift to the ♥J and hope declarer goes wrong.

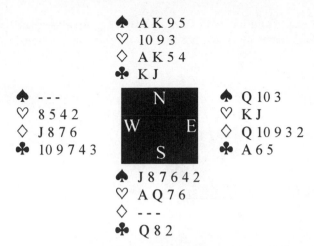

	♠ A K 9 5	
	♥ 10 9 3	
	◇ A K 5 4	
	♣ K J	
♠ - - -		♠ Q 10 3
♥ 8 5 4 2		♥ K J
◇ J 8 7 6		◇ Q 10 9 3 2
♣ 10 9 7 4 3		♣ A 6 5
	♠ J 8 7 6 4 2	
	♥ A Q 7 6	
	◇ - - -	
	♣ Q 8 2	

In the 1997 Cap Gemini World Top Tournament, Brazil's Gabriel Chagas shifted to the ♥J at trick 2. Fearing a singleton, declarer rose with the ♥A and now had to go one down.

2.

WEST	NORTH	EAST	SOUTH
	1♥	No	1♠
No	2♣	No	2◇ (1)
No	2♠	No	4♠
No	6♠	All pass	

(1) Fourth-suit forcing to game

Dealer North : East-West vulnerable. West to lead from:

    ♠ 8 5   ♥ 10 9 8   ◇ 8 7 6 5 2   ♣ K J 6

The normal lead would be a diamond, the unbid suit, but then you review North's bidding. The first two bids confirm five hearts and four clubs. 2♠, an unlimited bid since 2◇ was forcing to game, would show 3-card support but what do you read into the jump to 6♠? Combined with the failure to use Blackwood, the leap to 6♠ strongly suggests a diamond void. Not only will a diamond lead not give you any tricks, it might give declarer an extra trick in diamonds.

This is an unusual application of **DILLUS**. Dummy has length in hearts (perhaps six) and clubs is the suit that declarer might discard. Lead the suit where your tricks might vanish. Try the ♣6 in the hope of scoring two tricks before dummy's hearts can be used for discards.

The actual deal, from the 1997 Bermuda Bowl qualifying rounds, did not quite match the analysis, but the club lead worked in a curious way:

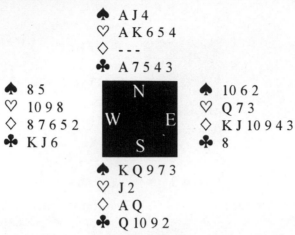

```
                    ♠ A J 4
                    ♡ A K 6 5 4
                    ◇ - - -
                    ♣ A 7 5 4 3
  ♠ 8 5                              ♠ 10 6 2
  ♡ 10 9 8          N               ♡ Q 7 3
  ◇ 8 7 6 5 2   W       E           ◇ K J 10 9 4 3
  ♣ K J 6           S               ♣ 8
                    ♠ K Q 9 7 3
                    ♡ J 2
                    ◇ A Q
                    ♣ Q 10 9 2
```

On a diamond lead, South would win in hand, draw trumps and set up the hearts before tackling clubs. When the hearts turn out to be 3-3, declarer can discard two clubs and make the slam with ease.

On a trump lead, declarer ducks in dummy and wins in hand, ruffs the ◇Q with dummy's ♠A, overtakes the ♠J in hand and draws the last trump. The hearts are tested next and when they prove to be friendly, declarer again does not need to try the clubs.

At three tables, West led the 6 of clubs. Fearing the lead to be a singleton, each declarer rose with the ace of clubs, drew trumps ending in dummy and led a club. One down.

3. Dealer West : Both vulnerable

```
  ♠ K Q 8 7 5       N               ♠ A 4 2
  ♡ 2                               ♡ K Q 8 3
  ◇ A K Q 10 8 7  W       E         ◇ 4 3
  ♣ 5                S              ♣ A 4 3 2
```

West opens 1◇, North bids 2♡ (a weak jump-overcall), East jumps to 3NT and West finishes in 6◇. North leads the ♣6. Plan the play.

Did you take the ♣A and ruff a club at trick 2? If so, well done. You are a **H.U.R.T.** disciple. The full deal:

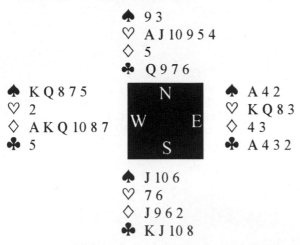

```
              ♠ 9 3
              ♡ A J 10 9 5 4
              ◊ 5
              ♣ Q 9 7 6
♠ K Q 8 7 5      N        ♠ A 4 2
♡ 2                       ♡ K Q 8 3
◊ A K Q 10 8 7 W     E    ◊ 4 3
♣ 5                 S     ♣ A 4 3 2
              ♠ J 10 6
              ♡ 7 6
              ◊ J 9 6 2
              ♣ K J 10 8
```

A heart must be lost, you can do nothing about a spade loser but you can cater for South holding ◊J-x-x-x by starting to reduce your trumps at trick 2. After ♣A, club ruff, ◊A, ◊K (revealing the bad split), you have to remove North's spade exits by cashing ♠K and ♠Q.

Then lead the ♡2. After North takes the ♡A, the position is:

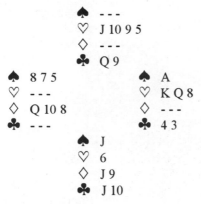

```
              ♠ - - -
              ♡ J 10 9 5
              ◊ - - -
              ♣ Q 9
♠ 8 7 5          ♠ A
♡ - - -          ♡ K Q 8
◊ Q 10 8         ◊ - - -
♣ - - -          ♣ 4 3
              ♠ J
              ♡ 6
              ◊ J 9
              ♣ J 10
```

North's exit is ruffed in hand. After a spade to the ace, play ♡K and ♡Q. If South ruffs, West over-ruffs and has the rest. If South discards, so does West and a club from dummy at trick 12 completes the coup. Brilliant!

INDEX